Living with Faith

Living with Faith

Barbara Butler

Copyright © Barbara Butler 2006

Cover image: Anne Gregson, 'Leap in the Dark'
www.littlewedlockgallery.co.uk

British Library Cataloguing in Publication data

A catalogue record for this book is available from the British Library

ISBN 1 85852 306 0

First published by Inspire
4 John Wesley Road
Werrington
Peterborough PE4 6ZP

Printed and bound in Great Britain by
Stanley L Hunt (Printers) Ltd, Rushden, Northants

Foreword

There have never been more compelling reasons for people of differing faith paths to engage with each other in new ways. Pressing upon us at every point of human life today is the need at least to understand how our global neighbours think and feel. Without knowing something of how *faith* shapes their self-identity we cannot possibly be true neighbours to them.

The London bombs in July 2005 were horrific, but part of a long and tragic series of global acts of terror and counter-terror. Equally shocking was the immediate reaction among far too many: the Muslim tradition was demonized as inevitably linked with viciously inhuman violence. Is it not the case, though, that we have all – believers and non-believers alike – been too prone to this kind of stereotyping? The more we learn of others' faith, the more we discover the amazingly diverse paths just one 'religion' takes. Yes, *jihad,* as the 'struggle' God expects of every true believer, is basic to Qur'anic faith, but how that struggle is understood and engaged in differs hugely. Being aware of these kinds of diversity within our faiths is an urgent need – for there are 'fundamentalists' within all faiths too who wish to exaggerate uniformities.

A related reason for greater understanding is the relentless push to global cultural uniformity, even within the lives of people whose traditions have been so very distinct. For a direct yet largely unexpected result of the pressures to join the modern, secular, global village and its monolithic markets is the violent polarizing of life in so many parts of the world. Everywhere we find intensified enmities as people's sense of self-identity, of what makes them distinct, is felt to be under threat. Most troubling is the danger of dominance by those with greatest power – economic, military, technological. And the destruction of people's cultural life is inherent in such global dominance.

There is, then, more urgent need than ever before for people of faith to relate in new ways to each other.

Relating in new ways is the key here. Many of us have long dreamt of one world, of greater human togetherness, increased cultural interaction and interdependence. Locally and globally we long for the peace that might flow from such new human togetherness. The reality, globally and often locally, is increased polarization, intensified enmities, greater conflict. Northern Ireland, Bradford, the Balkans, Palestine, Iraq/Iran, Chechnya, Uzbekistan, the Sudan, Nigeria, Kashmir, Sri Lanka, Indonesia – the list is almost endless. The one global village we dreamt of has become an apocalyptic nightmare. The way we envisaged the new world was deeply flawed.

And as Rome burns, Nero fiddles on, insanely ignoring the crucial factor in global human dynamics – our faith life. The western world (northern Europe in particular) usually assumes that a thoroughly secularist way of seeing things is normative. With nonchalant arrogance we either ignore the faith life of our global neighbours – as though the religious dimension of our humanness is irrelevant to our world's future life – or we make ignorant assumptions about what that faith means for human living. From any perspective, unbelief or faith, such arrogance is very stupid.

Or, is it *fear* of the other that is the primary problem? Is it the threatening strangeness of the other, the inbuilt tendency for the human psyche, personally and corporately, to demonize the other when passing through crisis-points in the process of shaping our human self-identity? Even if usually unrecognized, there are frighteningly destructive currents that flow within that identity-shaping process.

Christians, too, and especially those with clearly formulated and strongly held beliefs, all too often seem fearful of exposure to the faith of others. Faith in the greatness of Christ – surely – basic to being Christian – frequently and fatally seems linked to a demonizing of others' ways of faith and life. It is 'fatal' precisely because to fear the faith of others, even to lack all respect for others (including their faith life), is to be removed from that love of Christ in which 'all fear is cast out'. The arrogant ignoring of others' faith, equally, lacks the respect that love demands. No one can ignore the dearly held beliefs and practices of those they claim to love. And the respect that love demands must include a willingness to learn from others – not only to learn what their faith really means, but to be willing even to be touched by that faith.

For Christians, the most compelling reason to be interfaith people is the inescapable call to follow Christ faithfully. The Gospels witness to numerous incidents when Jesus speaks with striking respect for the faith of those not grounded in his own tradition. This Gospel witness shows Jesus being deeply touched by the reality of such faith.

What a tragic irony that it is often those seeming to be most ardent in following Jesus who most readily demonize people whose faith is other. Far too many claiming faith in Christ imagine they have to keep aloof from all faith that seems other than 'Christian'. Such exclusive forms of Christian faith are a dangerous part of the polarizing that threatens our world, God's world. For our faith is – precisely because we see life as 'in Christ' – in a God who created all, who lives and moves in all, who lovingly impinges on the life of all, who seeks the healing and peace of all, who 'illumines' all.

Barbara Butler's book provides a fine counter to fear, arrogance and exclusiveness. And it counters these in wonderfully wide-ranging ways. *Living with Faith* is such an apt title. It is, indeed, in *living*, in engaging with people whose faith is other, it is in learning just what that faith means within the lived humanness of others, that we move beyond fear. Such a learning process *may* entail quite deep immersion in the sacred texts of others. My own journey in following Jesus has led me to just such immersion in the faith life of others. Beginning as a lay preacher in rural Devon in 1950, eventually I was led to be a missionary in South India, there to be an interpreter of Hindu faith and culture for many years. It was a long engagement with the faith of others, and a pilgrimage that led to far greater awareness of what faith in Christ meant.

Engaging with love and respect in this way does not entirely rule out the 'cutting edge' of faith's convictions. Yet, only when there is deep inner engagement with others, deeply grounded empathy, can there also be a sharing in the self-critical reflection of others. Then, too, we become open to their critical reflection in relation to our own tradition. It is in this way that we learn to move beyond superficial tolerance of each other and into life-transforming friendship. Only then is there truly a 'living with faith'. Only then will we have really moved beyond those inherited, and alienated, identities that always keep us so distant from each other, moved on to a self-identity that is truly 'in Christ'.

Meanwhile, we have so much to learn from Barbara's account of innumerable instances from all over the world of the ways in which people have explored the wider meaning of their faith. We find here so many ways in which people have *lived out* their faith in new relationships with others, and thereby learned how to be more deeply rooted in that faith. God has many new things to teach us, and this book will help illumine the path of faith for many.

Eric Lott
Bruner Professor of Indian Religions,
United Theological College, Bangalore, India
Advent 2005

Contents

Introduction

Living with faith in the post-9/11 world

It is sometimes said that religion is like a knife. It can be used to cut down fruits from trees, to gather crops and to slice and butter bread. It can also be used to wound and even to kill. In the twenty-first-century world every person has a responsibility to meet people of faiths other than their own, to listen and to learn from those whose religion is a tool for living and for enabling others to live. It is only in this way that those who use their religion as a weapon to wound and to kill others can be challenged and ultimately stopped. And it is important to remember that wounding and destroying are not simply physical.

In July 2005 I organized a conference to give participants the opportunity to listen to stories of hope from Sri Lanka following the havoc wreaked by the great waves of the tsunami on 26 December 2004. There were encouraging stories about what is being done to rebuild homes and livelihoods but there were also stories of some religious groups taking advantage of the situation to try to build up their own communities. One example of this was of women in one area being told by a Christian group that if they joined the church they would receive sewing machines. The terrible result of this is that churches in that area, and in other areas where similar bribes have been offered, have been attacked.

I write as a British Christian who has met and worked with people of many faiths both in the UK and around the world for about 20 years. My book is mainly for Christians and it is written in the hope of encouraging more of them to meet and listen to people of other faiths than their own. I also hope that members of the other world faiths will read this book as part of their own inter-faith encounter. I am grateful for their friendship and for what I have learnt, of life and of the things of God, and of the unity of all things.

I write also for those people in western societies who do not practise a faith and whose initial awareness of people of other religions was largely post-9/11 when the religions were given a new prominence, though sadly they were mainly seen as sources of fanaticism and violence, as weapons of destruction. A Christian from Pakistan who travels regularly to England expressed the sadness and alienation he felt when after 11 September 2001 the British press was full of reports of Islamic fanaticism. This happened again following the 7/7 terrorist bombings in central London, but there has been a change which in other circumstances I would have called encouraging. After 7 July 2005 the reports were not only of the evils of Islamic fanaticism; there were also many articles and interviews with Muslims who abhorred the terror. Muslim lecturers are now in demand to explain their religion to many groups and organizations around the UK. Omar Bakri Mohammed, a former leader of the Islamist group al-Muhajiroun, was interviewed on television when he said that he would never tell the police if he knew of planned violence by Muslims. He left the country in August 2005 and leading Muslims came forward to say how relieved they were that he had gone. He was subsequently refused permission to return to the UK by the Home Secretary.

I write with urgency at a time when there has been a seismic shift in the way all religious faith is regarded, not only by the secular world in general but by political leaders in particular. Understanding religions is now seen as vital by the British government and by governments around the world. Many British police forces have recently appointed faiths officers and new recruits to the police service are now normally given courses to help them to understand the world faiths.

Religions are now firmly on the agenda, either as malign forces to be understood and overcome or as gatekeepers to deep wells of spirituality and the good values of peace, love and justice which every community aspires to.

I feel sure that in the post -9/11 and post -7/7 world meeting, talking, discussing and developing an understanding with people of other faiths is no longer an option for Christians, but a pressing and essential part of Christian responsibility. Communication with the secular world is also essential because ignorance of other faiths often leads to their marginalization and to the fuelling of divisions and hatred.

It was following the 9/11 tragedy that the then Archbishop of Canterbury, George Carey, invited a group of Christians and Muslims to Lambeth Palace for a high-profile two-day conference in 2002. The focus of the lectures and discussions was of the two faiths relating to each other, to God and to the modern world. The conference was an opportunity for a deepening of understanding between the members of the two faiths. A second conference was arranged, at Doha, Qatar, in 2003, when Christians and Muslims studied the Bible and the Qur'an together. The second conference took place under the cloud of the invasion of Iraq, which at least gave participants a sense of the urgency of their task of working for understanding and respect for each other, and of the need for shared communication of this with the world. This programme, which continues, is a sign of great hope.[1]

In August 2004 a sign of hope was sadly extinguished when a mural painted by Jewish children who were imprisoned in a World War Two concentration camp near Perpignan in southern France was destroyed by vandals. The Vichy regime had held 4,500 gypsies and Jews in the camp in 1941 and 1942 after which at least half of them died in Auschwitz, including 400 children. A Swiss nurse who looked after the children in the camp in 1942 had tried to divert them from their calamitous situation by asking them to create a mural of a typical Swiss scene on the wall of the infirmary. The mural was of the Swiss countryside and showed cows, chalets and forested mountains. It has now been destroyed beyond repair, probably by the use of a chisel. It is thought that what could have been mindless vandalism is more likely to have been antisemitic frenzy, following as it did other recent acts of antisemitism in the region and in France generally. The mural was to have been displayed in a memorial to the wartime prisoners. There is no wonder that many Jews are thinking of leaving France to live in Israel and that they are being encouraged to do this by the Israeli Prime Minister.

I have explored some of the divisions, sufferings and strife that have been fuelled by fear and ignorance of religions and by the people of faith themselves in Chapter 4. Ignorance and the prejudice it fuels must be confronted and changed on every level, beginning with the individual. I heard a talk by a Rwandan woman who escaped from being killed when the genocide was at its height in 1994 by running away and hiding. In her talk she said that it is mostly unhelpful if we think of over one million people being murdered in Rwanda. It is more salutary to remember that in Rwanda in 1994 one person was killed, and then another, and then another, and inexorably another, in what became a remorseless and seemingly endless succession.

The Bible teaches that God created all that is, including all of human life. Christians are challenged to see the light of God in all things and in every person, and thus to understand the overarching unity of the human race. Christians understand that the Christ is in and with all from the beginning, the divine reality for every situation and every person (John 1.4, 9).

This understanding might be illustrated by an unusual Christian community, but one now on the cutting edge of history. The Coptic Church is a community church in its homeland of Egypt and more recently around the world. It is a good example of a church and community that works out of the recognition that God is in all people and situations, serving them regardless of their religion or lack of it. In the Coptic tradition the Eucharistic bread is always round, symbolizing the world. In the middle of the bread is one big cross, surrounded by 12 other crosses, the 12 apostles. The cross is at the heart of the world, both a reality of life and a source of comfort in suffering, because it is not the end. It is there for the world and for all people as a sign of hope.

I have met Pope Shenouda, head of the Copts throughout the world, and he is very clear that to be a Christian is to embrace sacrifice for the sake of the whole world and its people. When he was asked how he manages to keep going in the face of attack and opposition he said with a smile that this was what it meant to be a Christian in the world today.

The Coptic cross is made, usually in a monastery or convent, by the plaiting of pieces of leather, during meditation on the interweaving of the cross of Christ into the world. It is a reminder that the Church can never exist in isolation from the world but must always be part of it, like the salt in the stew or the leaven in the lump. Such membership of the world may mean struggle and suffering, as it has for the Copts in some periods of their history, but it is a sincere living with the reality of life and of the presence of God.

I share with many people who have met seriously with people of other faiths the experience of the presence of God, both in the people and in the encounter, having received the loving service of people of other faiths on many occasions. I can never forget being welcomed into mosques and temples, into synagogues and prayer halls. One of my happy memories is of joining walking pilgrimages with people of all the major world faiths in London, when the Sikh people provided the food and fruit drinks from early morning until late in the evening. In 2005 about 300 people joined the pilgrimage, which has become an annual event organized by Westminster Interfaith. It is promising for the future that the interfaith walking pilgrimages have recently been taken up in other areas of the country.

Encounter with people of other faiths offers the opportunity to learn and to be inspired. I have not found it helpful to ask what impact a particular faith may have on me as a Christian. It is rather unrealistic to expect that a faith which people have been following for at least a lifetime, and through some of their traditions for several thousand years, may come alive to someone who follows another faith path. It is rarely possible for anyone fully to appreciate a faith without entering it and thus having the 'eye of faith'.

It is not even necessary for a Christian, or anyone else, in order to understand another faith, to like it or to agree with any aspect of it, though many people do come to appreciation and are sometimes able to look anew at their own faith, perhaps seeing in it facets that have not been very clear before their encounter with the other. I touch on this experience in Chapter 2.

A Christian may see what God is doing through the people of other faiths, and may learn about and respect their journeys. To do this it is essential to step into the unknown and then to move on to a recognition that the people of the other faiths are where they are because they are confident that they are in the right place. Trust in other people is essential for real encounter to take place. There must also be a willingness to listen on all sides. In this way there is no danger of a 'watering down' of any faith, for each unique religion will be presented as it is lived. Listening and sharing between people of the world faiths are the focus of Chapter 1.

People of faith who enter honest encounter with others will not deny the uniqueness of their own faith. Christians who enter encounter are, in sharing their faith, witnessing to the uniqueness of Christ without using that uniqueness as a threat. Witnessing to faith is the focus of Chapter 3. There are of course many examples, in Christian history and in today's world, of the use of bribes, threats and judgements to persuade others to become Christian. The story from Sri Lanka that I have included at the beginning of this introduction is but one example. Such approaches to other people are oppressive and lack respect. I believe that they are to be repented of and challenged.

My hope is that Christians enter relationships with people of other faiths in the trust that the Holy Spirit is at work in the others, in the encounter and in the outcome, which will be the result of each person or group's free choice. The entering and developing of any relationship is always a pilgrimage whose outcome is unknown. Pilgrimage, for those who are open and ready to experience the new and to learn from it, may lead to a new vision for life and even to a new life, though, as with any pilgrimage, the outcome can never be guaranteed. The vital thing is that people of faith embark on the pilgrimage with people of other faiths, and that they do so with respect, generosity and trust in the others.

The people of the Broadwater Farm Estate have travelled a long way since they were beset by racial troubles in the 1980s. The riots of 1985 caused two deaths and left people full of antagonism, frustration and anger. Since then a group of Christians has moved to live on the estate. They have lived and worked with the local people, including those of other faiths. A special effort has been made to honour the cultures of others, including literature, song and dance from all over the world. The atmosphere has been transformed and today the people of the faiths work together with confidence for interfaith and inter-racial harmony. For this to be possible someone had to take the first step.

On 9 May, 2004 a Spanish journey by people of faith took place that was remarkable, symbolic and faith-filled.

On 11 March 2004 Spain had suffered bombings on four commuter trains as they entered Madrid at the height of the rush hour. One hundred and ninety-two people had been killed and responsibility had been taken by al-Qa'ida, the motive being Spain's part in the Iraq war. National feeling was expressed against the atrocities and the national elections resulted in the government that had taken part in the Iraq war being defeated. The Spanish press focused on the lack of control of mosques and imams in Spain and on the dearth of knowledge of the Spanish Muslim community by the majority of the people.

Kathryn Lum has described the day,[2] when about a thousand people took the early Madrid train to Acala de Henares, the place where the people who were killed by terrorist bombs on 11 March had boarded the train. The train was very crowded and the carriages had stickers, 'Religions for Peace'. On arrival in Acala de Henares the pilgrims joined a silent walk to the university where there were readings from the world faiths, meditation and music. The challenge from the platform was to all the Spanish people to get to know people of other faiths than their own in the community, to develop trust and understanding and to work together for a faith-filled, truthful and peaceful future.

There is a tale in Olive Shreiner's *Story of an African Farm*, set in Cape Colony and published in 1883, of a hunter who, when he was hunting for wildfowl, reached a lake where an enormous shadow fell over him and he saw a dim reflection in the water. He was overcome by a longing to hold the large white bird, symbolizing truth, whose reflection he had seen in the water. He set off on his search. He left his home and travelled to unknown places, often going into danger. The years passed and he was old and dying on a strange mountainside. Just before he died a white feather fluttered down, and he died holding it.

1

Listening and sharing

There is an Asian tale of an old woman who longed to share her stories with other people, and who searched far and wide to find just one listener. She approached many people and asked them to listen to her, but they were all too busy and told her that they could not afford the time to hear her stories. Finally the old woman met a seller of salt and persuaded her to stop working to listen to the stories. Sadly, the young woman began to daydream and did not listen at all, but there was an unseen listener, who listened very attentively to the stories. It was the unborn child in the womb of the young woman. The unborn child gained great wisdom through listening, and was able to live a blessed and useful life.

It is not easy for many people of faith, including Christians, to be good listeners because we are all so keen to share our own faith, and so used to talking about it, that we often miss the opportunity to learn and also to share.

Formal efforts by Christians in the western world to be good listeners to people of other faiths have mostly been very recent, from about the middle or late twentieth century. This is not true of Christians in other parts of the world, especially in areas where they are a small minority of the people. We in the West have a lot to learn about listening and sharing from our Christian friends in countries where Islam is the majority religion, and in Hindu India, Buddhist Sri Lanka and many other areas.

It seems odd that many western Christians find it hard to be good listeners, because listening and sharing was at the heart of Jesus' ministry. He spent a lot of time with people from different backgrounds from his own, and some of them were those the 'religious' people had rejected, including the Roman centurion (Matthew 15), the

Canaanite woman at the well (John 4) and the Samaritan people.

Christian missioners, mostly from the West, did encounter people of other faiths in the nineteenth century and even earlier, but the majority tried to convert them, and when they mostly failed, they adopted negative attitudes. There were some exceptions to this approach to mission from the very beginning of the Church and increasingly in the twentieth century. I focus on issues of witness to faith in Chapter 3.

The first well-known occasion when people of faith gathered together to listen to each other from across the world was the World Parliament of Religions, held in Chicago in 1893. Most of the people who met were in fact Christians from many denominations, though some key members of other faiths also joined the gathering.[1]

Vivekananda, a Hindu and a disciple of the nineteenth-century mystic Ramakrishna, was perhaps the best-known person from a world faith other than the Christian faith to be present at the gathering. He spoke in Chicago and went on to set up the Ramakrishna Mission in 1897 and the Vedanta societies in Europe and America. The Vedanta societies studied Hindu advaitic, non-dualistic, philosophy through Vedic texts. Vivekananda saw God in all people and he saw his main challenge as helping people of faith consciously to make the link between meditation, study and service of others. He challenged people of faith to travel, internationally and also from village to village in India, to make others listen to them and to compel them to understand that sitting about idly would no longer be acceptable. He wrote about the faith path as the path towards increased awareness of God in all things and all people.

The 1893 Chicago gathering was sponsored by the League of Liberal Clergymen. They wanted to cooperate with people of other religions, rather than seek to convert them. The World Parliament of Religions took place just as a number of people of the world faiths were beginning to travel and live in the western world.

A well-known traveller from India in the late nineteenth century and the first half of the twentieth century was Rabindranath Tagore, the poet, novelist and artist who was born in 1861 and died in 1941. Tagore listened and learned everywhere he went and was well aware of himself as a natural part of the wide world from which he had everything to learn. He wrote:

> The same stream of life that runs
> through my veins night and day runs
> through the world and dances in
> rhythmic measures.[2]

Tagore did not always like what he heard and observed but both he himself and, through his writing and art, the whole of India and the world, were enriched by his learning. He received the Nobel Prize for literature in 1913.

Wherever he travelled Tagore always longed to be at home in his beloved Bengal though he was aware of God, the link of life, in every place and person. He wrote about his unease when he left home and his easy forgetting of the link between old and new places and of the overarching presence of God in every place. He knew that personal friendship and listening to God led to an awareness that there was no person who could ever be called an alien. The university of Santiniketan, founded by Tagore in 1921, is still both Indian and international, in its character and in the student and teaching community.

Mohandas K. Gandhi, a Hindu from Gujarat, also travelled to the West, and was a student in London in the 1880s where he developed an increased awareness of religion and philosophy by listening to a wide circle of people. It was at this time that he first read the *Bhagavad Gita* and Sir Edwin Arnold's *Light of Asia*. He also read the New Testament and was especially influenced by the

Sermon on the Mount. It was while he was in England that he met Quakers for the first time, though he had of course met many other Christians. The Quakers interested him in their faith and way of life. Gandhi's listening opportunities changed the course of his life towards his journey to sacrificial, non-violent actions of resistance to British rule in India.

A second World Parliament of Religions was held in Chicago, Japan and Bangalore in 1993. In the Japan gathering there was a Buddhist abbot whose predecessor had attended the 1893 gathering, a remarkable link.

The Chicago gathering was huge and included members of the world faiths and some of the new religious movements. There was a strong focus on the sufferings of the world. The Global Ethic, which I include as Appendix 2, was read for the first time at the final session of the Chicago gathering. It was an attempt by people of the world faiths to listen to people around the world, to respond to their troubles and sufferings, and to be committed to working more closely together to serve their world. This commitment to practical service was underlined when members of the world faiths gathered in Cape Town in 1999, when there was a call to the 'Guiding Institutions' of the world for action in four main areas: improving the plight of refugees; cancelling debt for developing countries; overcoming violence, especially when it was either motivated by religions or targeting religions; and increasing access to clean water. Everyone attending the gathering was asked to identify a 'gift of service' they could offer to the world. I touch on the 'gifts of service' in Chapter 5.

I attended the Bangalore gathering. The time together included a choice between visits to places of community and worship, workshops on issues facing the world faiths, and a study group on interfaith visions and cooperation. I will always remember the visit to the Sri Aurobindo ashram in Bangalore because it was beautiful and peaceful and also essentially practical. The students in the ashram, and in the main centre in Pondicherry, learn by listening, and then by meditating, thinking and practical work, including farming and engineering.

Sri Aurobindo, who himself moved from a very active political life into four years of silence in Pondicherry, dedicated his life from 1914 onwards to sharing his knowledge of God in all things and people. He believed that his sharing of the reality of God would lead others to awareness not only of God but also of God in all people, cultures and religions. He believed that such awareness would lead to cooperation, love and shared work.

Every day in Bangalore included worship, meditation and prayer. The evenings also included cultural programmes. I remember a special occasion when a Hindu classical dance group gave a performance that was focused, meditative and also beautiful. We moved from that experience to visiting a night shelter for street children.

It was only in the late twentieth century that the British churches began to recognize and work with people of other faiths as they became a growing presence in the major cities and towns.

In 1981 the British Council of Churches (BCC) published a booklet called *Relations with People of Other Faiths: Guidelines on Dialogue in Britain*. This booklet first introduced the four principles of dialogue, which were taken from the World Council of Churches' document, *Guidelines on Dialogue*. The General Synod of the Church of England supported the four principles in 1981. In 1984 a new booklet, *Towards a Theology for Inter Faith Dialogue*, was written and became a preparatory paper for the 1988 Lambeth Conference. In 1982 the Methodist Church reaffirmed its commitment to the four principles of dialogue. In 1983 the general assembly of the United Reformed Church adopted the guidelines. The original BCC booklet was revised in 1983 and sold 16,000 copies.

In 1991 I was involved in the publication of a new booklet, *In Good Faith: The Four Principles of Interfaith Dialogue: A Brief Guide for the Churches*. This booklet remains the latest official resource for individuals and churches who wish to get to know people of other faiths.[3] In the remainder of this chapter I deal in turn with each of the four principles of dialogue.

1 Dialogue begins when people meet each other

The people of the world faiths are ordinary people living in every city and in some of the towns and rural areas of the UK today, so it is not difficult in theory for Christians to meet them or for them to meet each other. The hardest hurdle to get over is the first one, the overcoming of shyness and the making of the effort.

The problem for many Christians in Britain is that they meet Christians when they go to church and for the rest of the week they tend to live rather compartmentalized lives, focusing on work and family. They do not necessarily relate religiously at all for most of the time, either with fellow Christians or with people of other faiths. If Christians think about other faiths it is likely to be in an academic way, not relating the faith to real people. They may in fact meet the real people in their everyday lives, walking around the local area and at their work, without registering that they are people of other faiths.

What is true of Christians is mostly true also for people of the other faiths, in that their lives tend to revolve around their families, their work and their place of worship and community, although, as I shall argue in Chapter 2, within their communities they are much more likely to live in a holistic way, with an awareness of God in every aspect of their lives.

When people of the world faiths come to live in Britain they are inclined to seek to live and work in places where people of their own faith already live and work. The Sikh community was first attracted to Southall in the 1960s when work was offered, and since then Sikhs have gathered for worship there from all over the world, even though recently many of them have chosen to live elsewhere. The Sikh places of worship in Southall are magnificent. There is also a Sikh secondary school and a sports centre.

When the Hindu people were forced by Idi Amin to leave Uganda in the early 1970s they gathered in the Midlands area and particularly in Leicester. Since then Hindus have gone to live in Leicester from Kenya and also from India. Leicester has also become a centre for the European Jain community, many of whom have gone there from East Africa and India.

I have arranged meetings between Christians and members of other faiths in Britain and around the world for about 15 years.[4] This has been very rewarding work as I have discovered that many Christians and people of the other faiths long to meet each other but are not sure how to go about arranging meetings. There are also those of all the faiths, sadly, who do not wish to meet people of other faiths at all. They are the ones we who do engage with others must spend time with, hard as it is to reassure them that they may listen to others and share with them without compromising their own faith and community.

Local initiatives to enable people of different faiths and communities to meet are growing. Councils or associations of faith exist in many areas now and most of them work hard to bring the faith groups together on a representative basis. Some of them, but not all, have a formal role, linked to the work of the local authority, while others are much more informal.[5]

The informal groups may meet in a home to learn about each other and about the faiths. It is impossible to know how many of these groups there are because they normally keep a low profile. Some discussion and study groups and many of the interfaith women's groups are in this category. Most of the informal groups have an open membership and deliberately avoid constitutions and other formalities. I have been a member of two interfaith women's groups, one in Birmingham and one in Leicester. The Birmingham group is linked in with the more formal Birmingham Council of Faiths, and puts on a conference for women every year. The Leicester group, of which I am still a member, is much more informal. It was initiated by myself and a Muslim woman and we began by inviting women of the major world faiths to join in. Members now invite others informally, though we try to keep the balance of the group and not to have too many people of one faith. The group is a wonderful way of sharing and learning. We have overlapping experiences of community life, of the stages of life and of pilgrimage. When a Hindu woman shared her pilgrimage to India, to a special place for people of her faith, she communicated something very spiritually significant for her which had obviously been an enormous physical effort. Listening to her became a spiritual experience for me and, I am sure, for other members of the group also. The recent work of this group has included the collection of a book of prayers and stories from the faiths for use in schools and interfaith groups.[6] At the end of this chapter I trace some of the stages in the development of some women's interfaith groups.

Other interfaith groups are more formal, with planned and published programmes, a membership fee and a constitution. There are now nearly 140 formal interfaith bodies in the UK, nearly half of which have been formed since 2000. Such groups often assume or are invited to take on a public role, including the organization of civic services and the preparation of advice on religious issues. They are becoming important now in promoting knowledge of the work for peace that their members are involved in internationally. Some of this work is referred to in chapter six. It is vital that the formal groups should be different from the informal groups, and should be truly representative of the faith communities in their area, thus including religious leaders as well as others. Currently the membership of the groups varies, with 42 per cent of the groups having corporate membership but the majority an individual membership.[7]

I feel that it is important that these formal interfaith groups do not take on a detached life of their own, which may be more likely when the membership is organized on an individual basis. To be of real value the members of formal groups should always consciously represent their own faith groups to the members of the other faiths and represent the formal interfaith group to the members of their own faith. It is only in this way that the minority of people who engage in interfaith dialogue may influence, challenge, and even change the majority who do not engage.

The Birmingham Council of Faiths has understood the value of being representative very well. It is aware of the need to be truly representative of the faiths in the area, whose delegates come together as equals, not compromising the distinctiveness of their faiths in any way. The council is also aware of the need to be a 'Council of Faiths' and thus recognized as a formal body by the city authorities and in the locality.

The Leicester Council of Faiths is also representative of the world faiths in Leicester and has a strong link with the City Council, which provides some funding.[8] The Leicester Council of Faiths was formed in 1986, so is one of the earliest councils to be formed in the UK. The first meeting was held on the initiative of the Lord Mayor and the tradition has developed of the City Council consulting the Council of Faiths on a whole range of important issues, including education. There is a varied programme of activities, all aimed at building a multi-faith and multicultural city, including the work with the City Council and the local schools, the university, the hospitals and the police. An important and creative new venture has been participation in the national and annual Holocaust Memorial, now held every year on 27 January. This has become an opportunity for many people of faith to come together across Leicester city and the county, to listen to history and to stories and music, to see works of art and to share visions for a peaceful future.[9]

Councils of Faiths may be linked through the Inter Faith Network for the UK.[10] The Network was established in 1987 to foster good relations between the different faith communities at national and local levels. Its membership includes bodies representing the major world faiths and national and local interfaith organizations and educational bodies with a focus on interfaith issues. All the member bodies of the Network have agreed to the document *Building Good Relations with People of Different World Faiths and Beliefs*. This document is an excellent guide for groups and individuals in listening, sharing and developing friendship with people of the world faiths.[11] It is included as Appendix 1 at the end of this book. I also refer to it in other chapters.

It is very encouraging to arrange groups, meetings and visits, especially when participants come to realize that the people of the faith they are meeting are in so many ways like themselves, each with the same human life, of happiness, sadness and challenge.

Owen Cole, who was to become a writer about the Sikhs, has described the time when he first attended *diwan* (worship) in the local Sikh gurdwara in Leeds. Here he met Piara Singh Sambhi for the first time, when he acted as his guide to the gurdwara. Owen was fortunate because he had met a Sikh who was very knowledgeable about his own faith. Owen asked many questions during his visit to the Leeds gurdwara which resulted in his being invited to Piara Singh Sambhi's home. Owen has explained that this was the beginning of a relationship of friendship and working together which lasted for over 20 years until Piara Singh Sambhi's death.

A simple visit to a place of community and worship, like the visit Owen Cole made, may lead participants to seek to learn more, to get to know the people, to read about and even to travel to other places associated with a faith. I often have requests for international pilgrimages and visits from people who have visited places of faith and community in the UK and who have been inspired by their experiences to learn more. I have enabled visits to pilgrim places of people of the world faiths which have given new insights to many of those who have taken part. Paul Kelly wrote of his visit to the Golden Temple in Amritsar:

> The Golden Temple of the Sikhs was a revelation, as a beautiful building and as a shrine. I was glad that we were able to go back in the evening to see the book being 'put to bed' with much religious fervour and the blowing of rams' horns. It was like the Ark of the Covenant – very Old Testament. Earlier we really did have a 'free lunch' along with hundreds of others.[12]

In meeting people of other faiths, both in the UK and across the world, many people become aware that what they thought they knew about the other faiths was not always quite accurate but was sometimes a series of stereotypical images created from what they had been told or had read.

When people meet people across the faiths, and once the initial shyness has been overcome, the learning and sharing is usually about ordinary human activity at first, but may then go on to include hopes and dreams, and sharing on the faiths themselves. Once the initial introductions have been made people are usually very happy to share something of their faith, and it then becomes clear that there are no stereotypes but simply people, who live and express their faith in their own way. It also becomes clear that there are many schools of all the world faiths, so that generalizations are not possible.

2 Dialogue depends upon mutual understanding and mutual trust

Understanding and trust may grow by simply living alongside people of other faiths, by doing things together as neighbours in the community, perhaps sharing the taking of the children to school, attending local meetings together, working for a new facility or enjoying a family or community occasion, a festivity or festival.

John Parry is a minister in the United Reformed Church. Through living and working in Southall and Manchester he has developed a love and appreciation of the Sikh people which he is very happy to share with others. John has learnt by living with the Sikhs and listening to them that they have much to teach him as a Christian about the way they recognize their dependence on God for his grace and go on to enjoy a unity of life in which their mystical experience is not divorced from their everyday living. The secular world is vitally important to them; it is part of their responsibility as people of faith. John has worked with Sikhs for many years, not least because he admires the way they are encouraged to fight for justice and truth in the world, bringing with them their spiritual insights and challenges. 'The history of the Sikh faith has demonstrated their willingness to strive for a just world to the extent that many Sikhs were willing to give up their lives.'[13] Participation in the special occasions and festivals of others, if it is done without criticism and is motivated by friendship and willingness to share and to learn, may be a very enjoyable way of beginning to develop understanding and trust.

Elizabeth Harris is the interfaith adviser for the Methodist Church and a student of Buddhism. She spent several years living and working in Sri Lanka and has described her attendance at the Perahera, the annual festival in Kandy in Sri Lanka, where thousands of Buddhist pilgrims go to watch the procession of the most sacred relic in their country, the tooth of the Buddha.

The focus of the procession is the ancient tusker elephant which carries, on his decorated back, a casket in which the tooth replica lies. Outside people are finding their plots on the pavement and spreading out sheets of plastic ready to wait for three or four hours ... Balloons, artificial flowers, candy, nuts, ice-cream, psychedelic sheeting and toys are being sold among the crowds ...

The boom of the cannon at an auspicious hour marks the beginning of everything. Processions from five places converge ... The procession is headed by whipcrackers ... After this come fire-throwers, dressed in black, wielding flaming sticks, dancing with burning thongs attached to their heads ... In the dark, the elephants, beautifully caparisoned and lit with strings of coloured lights, are a wonderful sight ... Before the procession began the pilgrims went to the Temple of the Tooth, to kneel in front of the tooth and to place offerings of flowers in front of the holy place.[14]

Understanding and trust may come through allowing the other person or people, of the other faiths, to explain their faiths from their own hearts and lives. People who are active members of churches are not good at listening to others, even when the others are Christians of another denomination than their own. An interdenominational gathering is always far more difficult to organize than a meeting of people of the same denomination. What is true of church members is even more true of ordained priests and ministers, who are trained to be speakers and teachers rather than listeners and learners. What is true of an inter-denominational gathering is even more true of an inter-faith gathering.

Mutuality is really the key to the development of understanding and trust between people. True listening, on both or on all sides, means each giving the other full attention, without interruption. Arguing, which so many of us who engage in dialogue love, is not helpful because it may, especially in the early stages of listening, destroy the confidence of one of the partners and thus make it impossible for true learning to take place. A person of faith must be free to define his or her own position, and this must be accepted as his or her position. This does not mean that it is or should be the position of the listener.

True listening involves vulnerability in the listener, because it must include the challenge of what is being said, and the possibility of being changed by it in some way. And then of course the listener becomes the sharer, and the roles are reversed.

It is only when people of the faiths speak to each other and are listened to by each other in an atmosphere of trust that any progress is made.

In the autumn of 2004 I shared the running of a course when Christians of all denominations listened to people of other faiths talking about what inspired them in their faith. Most of the speakers from the other faiths were not new to the Christian group. Some of them had introduced their faiths in earlier courses. The course on 'inspirations' was not an easy one to organize because it depended upon the speakers sharing something very personal and unique; it depended upon their becoming vulnerable to the listening group. It was only possible to run the course because there was trust between the listeners, who were very keen to learn, and the speakers, who knew that they were among friends. As the evenings went on the listeners became increasingly and visibly inspired by the enthusiasm and heartfelt inspiration of the speakers. Insights were given into the joy of learning from special religious leaders, the commitment and sacrifice arising from being members of faith communities, the joy of special festivals, the love of God gained through knowledge of the scriptures, the immense gratitude for the gift of grace and the holistic living made possible through regular daily meditation.

3 Dialogue makes it possible to share in service to the community

For work together in the community to be possible people of faith have not only to know and trust each other, but also to recognize that they do in some sense belong to the same community and that they have a shared responsibility for it.

The Chief Rabbi, Dr Jonathan Sacks, has written many times on his Jewish community.

> To be a Jew – our ancestors would have said – is to be born into a people whose story goes back to Abraham and Sarah. It is to be part of a covenant, enacted at Mount Sinai in the days of Moses, by which a group of recently liberated slaves pledged themselves to be 'a kingdom of priests and a holy nation'.[15]

The Jewish community is much more complicated today, following its long history of struggle, diaspora, division and rejection, and it continues to struggle for existence in many countries although it is strong in others, including Britain. Referring to the renaissance in the Jewish community at the beginning of this century, Jonathan Sacks wrote:

> People want to belong. They feel lifted by knowing that they are part of a tradition. They welcome the chance to be part of a community, giving to others and knowing that others will be there for them should the need arise.[16]

Because members of communities feel protected and secure they also feel free to express themselves honestly and sometimes to criticize other members. Internal quarrels and struggles may occur frequently, but they are the quarrels of those who ultimately put the community before themselves and are therefore prepared to compromise their principles and even, on occasions, not only to make sacrifices but also to give in.

The sense of community exists in all the world faiths. In Islam the *ummah*, the worldwide community of the faithful, brings all Muslims together, which is a special privilege and also a responsibility. The community of all Muslims, said to be more than a billion worldwide, transcends all other loyalties even though the members of the community are very different from each other in education, culture, social status and standard of living. Muslims include the richest and the poorest people in the world. A Muslim woman called Nasreen wrote about her pilgrimage to Mecca, the journey which unites all Muslims:

> I think we're lucky being in Europe ... we have work, a job that pays us quite well ... It's far too easy for us ... We'll travel on the coaches, but those people who come from poorer countries, they'll sleep rough, they'll eat little and they'll even walk from one place to another. Yeah, so I value those people's Haj more than ours.[17]

The Sikh religion is based on a firm belief in the equality of all people and in the responsibility people have to worship and eat regularly as a community. 'The highest and most beneficial deed is the Lord's praise in the holy congregation.'[18] Arrangements for daily morning and evening worship exist in most gurdwaras but Sunday is the day when the whole community gathers together. The Sunday services vary but include prayers, songs, talks, poetry and music. The service will end with the recitation of prayers and the sharing of the *karah prashad*, cooked semolina, sugar, water and ghee or clarified butter. The sharing of the *prashad* is symbolic of the unity and equality of the people, who then share a meal together in the *langar* or dining room. Sikhs are always aware of and accepting of the people of other faiths.

> The Universe is burning
> Be merciful O God.
> By whatever path anyone approaches you,
> Lift him and accept him.[19]

Jonathan Sacks first introduced the phrase 'community of communities' as a helpful way forward for people of the world faiths, who are all as much part of their own communities as the Jewish people and are also part of the huge community that comprises all people of faith. The real struggle of every person occurs when the demands of one community do not simply overlap with another but clash in a very challenging way.

Dilwar Hussain is a research worker at the Islamic Foundation at Markfield. He gave a series of talks at one of the 'Faith Awareness' courses run by Christians Aware. He spoke about the nature of Islam and the struggles faced especially by young Muslims who are being brought up in Britain today. They have huge questions hanging over them. Are they British or Pakistani, Bengali, Gujurati or Middle Eastern? Are they members of their families first or are they part of Britain's youth culture? If they are still at school, which school is the centre of their lives – their day school, perhaps the local comprehensive, or the evening *madrassah* that teaches the faith? How can they be British and also loyal to their faith? There has been a spotlight on young Muslims since the 7/7 bombings in central London. Many of them have been interviewed and asked whether their country or their faith came first. The answers have been varied.

In 2000 the Commission on the Future of Multi-ethnic Britain, chaired by Bikhu Parekh, used the phrase 'community of communities' as a tool to describe how Britain could be seen at its best.[20]

The Commission pointed out that Britain has never been a monochrome society, but that there have always been internal differences and tensions between the classes, the regions, between men and women and between those of different political views. The growth in the numbers of people of many faiths added another category of difference, but it certainly did not create difference. Most Christians who experience dialogue and friendship with people of other faiths would agree that the presence of the people of other faiths simply strengthens the community of those who recognize a transcendent God and who seek to love and work for the world and its people.

The Commission pointed out that, as in the past, so today, communities overlap with each other and therefore inevitably influence each other. Every person belongs to two, three or more communities, places where they share the same story, the same symbols and ceremonies: where they feel at home, trusted and understood, loved and respected, listened to and listening. As members of the communities they also have a love and responsibility for the other members and are prepared to make sacrifices for them and to share with them in responsibility for building peace and justice.

In Chapter 5 I introduce work that is shared by members of the world faiths. I find this work inspiring and a huge sign of hope for the future of our one world.

4 Dialogue becomes the medium of authentic witness

'Witnessing to faith' is the focus of Chapter 3. It tends to be the women who keep the unity of faith and culture alive in the UK today, as they do everywhere in the world. Women's interfaith groups are a recent development in the UK. They are difficult to set up and harder to keep going, but if they survive they may be spirit-filled and supportive communities. Many women's interfaith groups pass through the four main stages of dialogue, of meeting, developing trust, working together and sharing faith.

Most meetings between women of faith occur simply and naturally. I met someone who became a very good Hindu friend when we were lecturers together in the same college in Zambia. At first we had teaching in common and an interest in African history and culture. Gradually we met each other's families and began to discuss our faiths and ways of living. I was invited to Hindu cultural evenings and met and developed friendships with many people in the Hindu and Sikh communities in Lusaka.

Many primary and secondary schools in Britain's large cities and in an increasing number of towns are made up of children from many of the world faiths and the mothers meet each other as they collect their children from school. 'David is going to play with Samar,' one mother said to me, and she went on, 'I think they may be Muslims, because they are fasting at the moment, but I haven't asked them.'

Other meetings take place at work or through families living near to each other. I used to visit a community of Roman Catholic sisters in Southall, whose members got to know the people of other faiths simply by living near to them. One of the sisters organized sewing groups and another organized study and discussion groups. The women of all faiths in the neighbourhood came to the groups. The courses on interfaith issues run by the sisters were well supported by people of all faiths. I met women from many backgrounds during the courses, a Buddhist nun, a Sikh woman who was a school inspector, a Muslim woman who led classes in meditation, and many more.

The most natural meeting between people of faith is when they are brought up together and are thus able to relate as trusted friends in adulthood. Jeanne Kattan, a Palestinian Christian in Israel, spoke about her upbringing at a conference for 'Christians in the Holy Land' in 1993. She said, 'I speak Arabic and have something in common with all Muslims ... I have nothing against Jews ... I have shared my life with Muslims, at home and in school.'

I have already written a little about the struggles faced by many young Muslims in Britain today. There is now a generation of young adults of most of the world faiths in Britain who were born and brought up together and who have a loyalty to each other, and who struggle with this when it clashes with their families and faith communities.

Women's interfaith groups are growing in number in the UK and around the world. Most of them are hard to organize, especially in the early stages, and they often rely on their informality, so that members do not feel obliged to attend, because faith, family or work usually have priority. In the early stages of groups, when women are meeting for the first time, many of them try very hard to explain their own faith to others, but find it difficult to listen. Many women are much more loyally defensive of their faith than most men. They are normally the guardians of the faith, the ones who practise it in the family and who link it to culture and tradition, seeing it very clearly as the future through bringing up their children. This may be a tremendous strength but it may also become a weakness if it builds walls instead of bridges between one faith and the others.

The women's interfaith groups whose members do move on to develop trust in each other are usually those that allow time and space for members to get to know each other in a relaxed way. Shared meals and informal conversation are important, so that people begin to learn about each other's families and work and come to realize how much they all have in common.

When the formal discussions do begin they are not easy at first, and may involve long and wooden conversations when members of the different faiths tread very carefully in getting to know each other. Some groups plan an event early in their development as a way of bringing people together. I have already referred to the Birmingham group which chose the task of arranging an annual conference early in its life. The subjects of the conferences included 'Faith, Family and Community', 'Women, Faith and Wholeness', and 'Women of Faith challenged by the Millennium'. The conferences have grown over the years and are now very popular. They include women of many of the main world faiths, and they are the first opportunity most of them have had to take part in such a day. Participants have spoken about having their minds opened by the surprising experience of learning something new from someone of another faith, of seeing life and the world from another point of view. One woman said, 'I really feel encouraged about the possibility of a better world now, of all faiths, I met so many committed people.'[21]

I asked a member of the Concord Women's Friendship Group in Leeds to write about the development of her group. She wrote:

> It all began when a car load of women, including a Sikh, a Hindu, a Jew and a Christian, attended a day conference for women of all faiths in Birmingham. We formed a small group of active women, including Baha'is, Brahma Kumaris,[22] Buddhists, Christians, Hindus, Jews, Sikhs, Muslims and a brave pagan. The group worked hard to organize two interfaith women's conferences in Leeds and both were well attended.[23]

One of the most effective ways to develop trust is for groups to arrange visits to each other's places of community and worship. A women's group, made up mainly of Christians, visited a Sikh gurdwara in Southall, where they received generous hospitality. Two participants wrote about this afterwards and were obviously impressed by the feeding programme for five or six hundred people every day of the week.

The visitors were taken into the prayer hall where women were leading the singing and reading from the Sikh holy book, the Guru Granth Sahib. The discussion between the visitors and the host community focused on women's responsibility in Sikhism, in every aspect of life, in the home, in service to the community and in worship.

At the heart of the Sikh faith is the belief that religion cannot be separated from life and that the religious person must offer service to the community. Work for others is an essential part of faith and, as we have seen, if such work is shared by people of more than one faith it is one of the best ways of enabling understanding and friendship. This is true for women of faith who have learnt to trust each other as much as for groups of men and women working together.

The Leicester interfaith women's group has shared the joint project I have already touched on of gathering together prayers and stories for use in school and community worship.

In one community I work with in Calcutta, Christian, Hindu and Muslim women come together to educate the pavement children. The teachers are involved with the parents as well as the children in pavement schools, which are literally on the dusty pavements, in primary schools where the pupils meet after dark when the fee-paying pupils have gone home, and also in secondary schools, from which some of the children go on to universities. One of my friends is a Hindu woman, a member of the Ramakrishna Community in Calcutta, who has given up a promising professional life to teach Muslim girls who would not otherwise have an education. Through her love and service for those who are of a different faith from her own she has become a bridge-builder between the faiths.

Another women's group working for education is the Palestinian Women's Network of Muslim and Christian women. The network focuses on young women between the ages of 15 and 24, to help them to complete their education. They give special care to women in rural areas and to the development of children, so that they may, hopefully, grow up without hatred. The workshops run by the network include: polygamy, early marriage and divorce, crisis management, coping with fear and anxiety, activating women's roles under siege, empowering women through the internet, shelter for abused and mistreated women and a radio station and TV programmes.

Muslim and Christian women worked together to help to bring peace in Bradford, during and after the riots of June 1995. They were able to do this because they had met together regularly, in each other's homes, to share news and concerns about local and wider issues. On 9 June 1995 four young men were arrested and the crowds gathered. Attempts at mediation by the community leaders broke down and fires were lit and shops damaged. There were more disturbances the next day and that night eight Muslim and Christian women walked together through the troubled area carrying candles and a banner for peace. This action had such an impact on the crowds of people that the night ended peacefully for everyone.

The United Nations' fourth conference on women was held in Beijing in 1995 when the delegates focused on practical issues including the need for primary health care, clean water and sanitation for women and their families. They also discussed human rights and issues of war and peace. In working together the women from around the world, of many faiths and of none, gradually came together as friends. The Arab delegation to the conference included Christian and Muslim women who are continuing their shared work long after the conference is over. In Britain the Baha'i women have been the leaders in keeping the issues of the conference alive and in calling women of all faiths together in regular groups.

When women's groups do persevere towards trust and working together their members are often able to be very honest with each other about faith. They no longer try to promote their own faith, but are able to share their history and personal experiences honestly and openly even when they are painful or frustrating. A Jewish friend gave me a book to read about the time her father spent in a ghetto in Lithuania. I read the book and wrote a review but when I wanted to discuss the stories in the book my friend told me that she had not read it because she knew that to do so would be too painful. I was shocked as I realized that, for those who remembered, the horrors of the Holocaust were just as terrible now as they had been 60 or more years ago.

I was also taken by surprise, though in a happier way, when a Muslim friend asked me to say the Lord's Prayer at an interfaith women's group. We had journeyed a long way together when the request was made and it was an important moment in the life of the group, a moment of hope and commitment to the continuing journey together.

The only listener to the wise old woman in the story was the unborn child, but such attention is possible for every person who is prepared to focus and to give time. It is possible to engage with people of other faiths than our own on levels of listening, sharing, dialogue and meditation. As the relationship moves from dialogue to meditation it may also move from focusing on differences between the faiths to what they have in common, to shared experiences and values.

Rabindranath Tagore wrote in his *Gitanjali*, his song offering to God:

> Thou hast made me known to friends
> whom I knew not. Thou hast given me
> seats in homes not my own. Thou hast
> brought the distant near and made a
> brother of the stranger.[24]

2

Wholeness and holiness

There is a Sufi story told by Rumi, of a rich pleasure-seeking prince called Ibrahim. While Ibrahim is out hunting deer, he is separated from his companions. Suddenly, as he sits on his horse in the vast and lonely forest, he hears a voice speaking to him and he hears the message three times:

Ibrahim, I did not create you for this. Is this the best you can do with your life?

When Ibrahim sees a shepherd he dismounts and takes off his beautiful clothes and jewels and gives them to the shepherd. He puts on the shepherd's rough clothes and vows to leave his palace. He sets off, telling his friends that he will search the whole world to discover why God created him.

Rumi ends the story by pointing out that Ibrahim had made great efforts to catch the deer, but had instead been caught by God. He had begun his lifetime journey towards holiness and there was no inconsistency in his day-by-day living along the way.

Today western Christians do not necessarily associate holiness with wholeness of life, unlike many of their sisters and brothers in the developing world and in the other world faiths. The western world, industrial, urban and business-orientated, has long tended to compartmentalize life, so that time spent in church on Sunday, if time is spent there at all, does not necessarily link in with the way time is spent for the rest of the week, at work and in the family. This has not always been the case.

Jesus was a great bridge-builder between his Jewish community and the communities of people he and they lived among. Sometimes he pioneered the bridge-building by making personal connections which others could follow.

When Jesus met the woman at the well he met with a woman who was seen as unclean by the Jewish people, a Samaritan woman. Jesus should not, according to the traditions of his people, have spoken to her, let alone have asked her for a drink of the polluted water. But he did speak, and he focused his full attention on her, seeing her as a real, true person, even though she had a questionable lifestyle, and, moreover, he asked her to help him. He gave her the gift of giving.

Jyoti Sahi is a well-known Indian artist, living in an ashram near Bangalore. Jyoti has painted the woman at the well many times. One of the paintings I have seen shows Jesus as an eastern holy man, towering over the poor woman at the well. But the woman is painted in blue, and is part of the water springing out of the well. She is the one giving Jesus new life, new hope. She is the one who is serving him, and she is the one bringing the things of God to him.

The Hebrew Bible and the New Testament are full of stories of bridge-building. One of the stories in the Hebrew Bible is the story of Ruth, set in the time of the Judges and written down after the Babylonian exile. Ruth was a Moabite woman who married an Israelite who then died. She, contrary to all tradition, stayed with Naomi, her mother-in-law. She has thus always been celebrated as a bridge-builder between peoples, and as an example to people of all faiths.

The early Celtic Christians in Britain saw no separation between their prayer lives and their everyday lives. They prayed to God who was with them in their homes and in the fields, in their every activity from getting up in the morning to going to bed at night. The early monks and nuns underlined this understanding of God in all of creation. They built no barriers between the monasteries and the outside world. The monasteries were the centres of the communities they sprang up in. The monks and nuns went in and out naturally and so did the lay people, rich and poor alike. Later monasticism was not so relaxed but it did put ordinary life, work and worship together on an equal level, growing from both Celtic monasticism and the rule of St Benedict.

After the Norman conquest of Britain the cathedrals and some parish churches assumed the central role in the communities of the new dioceses. To some extent this tradition has also developed in the Roman Catholic and Lutheran Churches in much of mainland Europe and in the post-Reformation Anglican Church in England. Martin Luther helped people of his day to see work as a vocation. He said that ordinary work in the community, serving the people, however simply, was a calling from God which was as important as the life of the monk in the monastery. An Anglican congregation in England at the beginning of the twenty-first century will understand its responsibility to the geographical area of the parish, including homes, shops, schools and places of work. The problem is that the responsibility of the congregation has often been translated into the responsibility of the priest, thus becoming part of the affliction of compartmentalism.

The approach to life as a unity of living, working and praying, with constant awareness of God in everything, is at the heart of Christian life in much of the non-western world today. I have experienced it in many African countries where people and priests feel, and in reality are, equally responsible for the churches and for the love and care they give to the surrounding communities. Services are often very long, because people are relaxed into them and their real selves and their everyday lives are there, because there is no division.

This unity of living with God in every moment of day and night is still taken for granted in many of the communities of most of the great world faiths. It is because members of the world faiths are now a permanent part of the western world that there is the opportunity for western Christians to learn something about a unity of living, wholeness and holiness, which was once central to their own traditions. Learning is not easy, however. As I touched on in Chapter 1, we all find it hard to go into new communities for the first time and it is even more difficult if the communities are of people of another faith than our own, a faith we may either struggle to understand or not wish to know or learn about at all.

A good example of the achievement of faith and wholeness of life can be seen in the story of a young Hindu woman who was born in East Africa, brought up in Coventry and is now married to a Welsh agnostic. She has spoken about her life and faith and they are a unity. Neera Vyas is grateful for her traditional Hindu childhood because it has given her stability and rootedness even though she has moved about so much. She now describes herself as a modern Hindu woman, keeping statues of gods and goddesses in her home and worshipping, not the images, but, through right thought, right living and meditation, the one mysterious Godhead.

I realize that it is very difficult for those of us who are members of one faith to know and appreciate another faith. There are of course the notable exceptions, people who are great mystics and great scholars. Most people, however, do not have as much time as they would wish to explore their own faith, let alone to begin to get inside another faith.

As I have touched on in Chapter 1, it is possible for many people to begin to appreciate and learn from individuals and communities on a number of levels, beginning perhaps with occasional attendance at festivals and visits to places of worship and community. There is also, in the midst of all the divisions in the world today, the very infrequent emergence of a rare gift, in the shape of an inspiring person or event, which may serve to bring people together. Amir Khan, the 17-year-old Muslim Olympic boxer from Bolton in Lancashire who won a silver medal for Great Britain in Athens in August 2004, was such a gift. The people of Bolton, of all the faiths and backgrounds there, were proud to claim him as their own. There was an atmosphere of amazing unity and pride in Bolton and its people, both during and after the Olympic Games.

There is the popular leisure time enjoyment of places of culture and relaxation, including the many restaurants that are springing up in the major British cities. Bradford is a good example of a city that has successfully sought to attract tourists through its Asian community of the Muslim, Sikh and Hindu faiths.

Komal Patel and Hena Mistry, both aged 14, have written about Hinduism as one of the world faiths in Leicester.

> There are many places for worship, mosques, churches, gurdwaras and temples ... A good place to look for evidence of Hinduism in Leicester is in the Belgrave area. The well-known shops in the Melton Road have it all ... A prime example of this is the underground cash-and-carry. As soon as you walk in, there is a section full of statues of gods (*murtis*) ... The shop has cards that can be used for any occasion ... There is a whole section on music.[1]

Some Christians say that they are closer to Judaism and Islam than to the other world faiths, because Judaism and Islam were formed in the same part of the world and share some common history. Shared discussion and work between members of the three faiths have, however, very sadly been reduced since 9/11 and since the London bombings of 7 July 2005. I explore the implications and some of the outcomes of 9/11 and 7/7 elsewhere in this book, mainly in Chapter 4. At this point it is important to remember that both days of terror and death prompted many interfaith meetings, prayers and acts of solidarity all over the world. The 7/7 London bombings spurred the nation into a two-minute silence that was observed by people of all faiths.

Christianity, Judaism and Islam have all developed within the Semitic tradition and were also influenced by the Greek world. They point to an uncompromising belief in one God. They have a linear view of history, in which people move from birth to death and the beyond. The history of the faith is central, the written scriptures are vital and God is utterly beyond and separate from the creation. The Council of Christians and Jews and the more recently formed Three Faiths Forum are organizations based on the understanding that Christians, Muslims and Jews have much to share and to learn from each other. This approach makes it possible for some members of the three faiths to work together for greater understanding and for causes they can all support even though this working together is now harder than it used to be.

There is an inspiring story from young people of the Christian, Muslim and Jewish faiths in Nottingham. The young people in a church youth group were studying the story of Noah and realized that this story was shared by the Jewish and Muslim people. They contacted Nottingham Inter Faith Council and organized a series of sessions with Jewish and Muslim young people. The Noah theme was approached through art, music and role-play. Lucy, one of the participants, explained that the art, music and role-play enabled the young people to get to know each other.[2]

The disadvantage of Christians, Muslims and Jews making common cause is that people of the eastern faiths may feel very unappreciated in today's multicultural Britain, because their faiths, including Hinduism, Buddhism, Jainism and Sikhism, were formed in a different part of the world and had a different development, with different understandings of God and different expressions of faith and culture, within the Indo-European tradition.

Hinduism is perhaps the hardest world faith for a western Christian to understand and learn from. It has developed with a recognition of the possibility of one God who may be known in many forms, with a cyclical view of life and reincarnation, and with an understanding of the divine presence in all things. Many Christians find it very hard to enter a Hindu temple, where everything is strange and even unattractive to them. One man who gave a talk at a conference I attended described his first entry to a Hindu temple in west London. When he entered the bright and shining temple he was in total shock, partly, he later realized, because the temple was the polar opposite of his own local Anglican church. Sometimes, as on this occasion, dislike and misunderstanding of the outer appearances in a temple may lead new visitors to question and reject the integrity of the life and faith they have only just begun to glimpse. It is important not to forget, however, that Orthodox, Roman Catholic and many Anglican Christians are used to pictures, images, bells, light, flowers and incense in their worship, and some of them may have easier access to Hinduism than Christians of the more Protestant traditions.

Knowledge and appreciation of the wholeness and holiness present in the members of the world faiths is easier for most of us in one particularly powerful way. An experience that E. M. Forster had may be a key to opening an unfamiliar door into a fresh way of looking at the world faiths, through their practitioners. Forster travelled in India when he was preparing to write *A Passage to India*. He wrote down some of his exposure in *The Hill of Devi*,[3] from which the reader will gather that he did not like Hindu temples, which he saw as far too bright and garish to appeal to his muted English tastes.

After a while, during one particular visit to a Hindu temple in India, E.M. Forster realized that his dislike arose because he was looking in the wrong direction and asking the wrong questions. He came to an awareness that he should not have been looking at the images, the decoration or even at the ritual. He should not have been asking what these places and the rituals did for him. He should have been looking at the faces of the people. He should have been asking what the places, the images, the decoration and the rituals did for them, for those who followed the path of faith, for those with the eye of faith, the Hindu people.

E.M. Forster came to realize that any enrichment, appreciation and understanding a Christian may receive by visiting a Hindu temple will not normally come directly from the faith itself, but will come through watching the people and appreciating the holiness and wholeness in their faces and in their total absorption in their worship, sometimes leading to contemplation and taken out into every aspect of life.

It is largely, then, through the people themselves, the Hindu pilgrims, that Christians may, given time and the development of trust, come to some understanding of the Hindu faith in its great variety. Through meeting Hindu people Christians will begin to notice that they are not all alike in their approach to their faith and that generalizations about them are not appropriate. Meetings with the people may lead to a study of the faith, to awareness of schools of philosophy and to further appreciation and enrichment.

When David Clark joined a Sikh pilgrimage to the Punjab in the autumn of 2004 with a Christians Aware group he had a different experience. The group spent time meeting people in their homes and visiting places of work and community. They learnt about history and spirituality, they joined early morning meditation and visited many gurdwaras. A highlight of the visit was when the group went to the Golden Temple in Amritsar. At five o'clock in the morning they joined the procession, walking clockwise around the sacred pool to the causeway, to honour the arrival of the Guru Granth Sahib. They crossed the bridge and found that the verse for the day, from the Guru Granth, was pinned up.

> He alone is called warrior, who is attached to the Lord's love in this age.[4]

When David entered the Golden Temple he found that his lifetime of Christian living and working immediately linked to his pilgrimage amongst the Sikhs in their holy place. He wrote:

> In the Golden Temple I remember thinking this is a universal experience of holiness: walking through a holy place with countless pilgrims, intent on making contact with divinity. No matter the language, no matter that the relationship between Christianity and Sikhism is a largely unexplored region, the sense of goodness and devotion all around was present and almost palpable. I felt my own trust in God strengthened, as I sensed the love of God in these calm, respectful crowds.[5]

A wonderful example of wholeness and holiness may be found in a description of home life by a member of a Hindu family living in Oxfordshire. Chandra Vadivale was born in Malaysia, came to the UK as a student in 1971 and married in 1979. He has written:

> From this point on, wherever we have lived, there has been a permanent prayer space ... In 1985 we moved to our present house, chosen mainly for its outbuilding which we could convert into a private temple ... At the same time our family was growing ... but whatever changes were made, religion was always the core of our family life ... we should always recognize and serve God in every aspect of our home and family life ... There is no point in giving a child every material advantage and neglecting to teach

him or her how to worship God ... The prayer room is the heart of the Hindu home.[6]

There was a growing awareness of the strength of faith and community leading to a growing realization of God as a member of the family, not taken for granted but nevertheless ordinary and ever present in every situation of good and ill. Chandra Vadivale writes, 'The first person in the home is always God.'[7] I have been invited to Hindu temples in the UK and also in India, Sri Lanka and Mauritius and have been given a warm welcome which has led to further meetings and invitations, further opportunities to learn.

Visiting the homes of people of other faiths often makes clear the unity of life and faith which they enjoy. This is sometimes seen in the strong links between the very old and the very young, and in the respect the young have for the old, which I have already referred to. I experienced this respect in a different setting, when I was invited to a series of plays in an inner-city school. The children had written their own plays and the central theme was how the old people could be cared for now that the families are living in western cities, surrounded by a culture of division and the marginalization of the elderly.

In one of the Leicester temples on one occasion I stayed for a long time, listening to the chanting and watching the rituals and people. There was an old man who was totally absorbed in the worship. Afterwards I was introduced to him and invited to visit his home. When I went to his home a few weeks later I found a place of welcome and love. The family lived in a small and narrow street behind the temple and the door was open to friends and neighbours at all times. The children of the next-door family came in when they arrived home from school and they were given a blessing. The discussion was about the temple and about their great devotional book the *Bhagavad Gita*, which everyone read every day.

I found that I could begin to learn about the most popular of the Hindu scriptures through listening to people who honoured it as their main inspiration and source of wisdom and also as their link to the transcendent. I discovered that I wanted to read the *Bhagavad Gita*, and when I did I found it uplifting and inspiring. I also began to see some areas of my own Christian faith in a new light.

In the second chapter of the *Bhagavad Gita* the Lord Krishna advises Arjuna, who is fighting a battle, to see God as a partner in the whole battle of life and to work with God for the sake of the work itself, and without any selfish wish to be part of any future outcome.

> But thou hast only the right to work, but none of the fruit thereof. Let not then the fruit of thy action be thy motive; nor yet be thou enamoured of inaction.

> Perform all thy actions with mind concentrated on the Divine, renouncing attachment and looking upon success and failure with an equal eye. Spirituality implies equanimity.[8]

The New Testament is full of stories from the world of work, the ordinary world that was the setting for Jesus of Nazareth's everyday life. Jesus taught that work should not be done in isolation from everything else, but rather it should be lived as a natural part of the process of getting to know God. The good shepherd gave everything he had, even his life, for his sheep, his work, and this was also his giving of everything to God.

Christians and Hindus, and indeed members of the other world faiths, are taught that work and worship go together and that when they are thus yoked it becomes possible for work to be done in a spirit of detachment and unselfish love. Work thus becomes the pilgrimage. It becomes possible for the spiritual seeker to live with the faith that God is in all things and people and to come to understand that work is worship and worship is work.

There is no separation and no conflict. The Celtic Christians were among those who knew this. Vivekananda knew this and, as we have seen, constantly travelled and worked for people of faith to make the link between meditation, study and service of others.

Meetings with people of faith may develop into deep levels of listening, sharing, dialogue, worship and meditation for every person who perseveres. There are many people of faith who are ready to share with Christians, so long as the Christians are prepared to take time. It is only when time is taken that delight in the depth and richness of faith and in the oneness of this with everyday life may be appreciated.

In the summer of 2004 Christians Aware arranged a number of visits to places of worship of people of some of the world faiths and in each place we listened to a talk on meditation and then meditated. People were delighted to share the richness of their traditions and their experiences. We learnt from Sikh, Hindu, Buddhist and Quaker speakers, all seeking the unity of life and the transcendent which would bring not only peace, but also increased usefulness in the world.

Brother Nicholas Allen of the Society of Saint Francis has written about his long encounter with Buddhists and with Buddhism. He has described his weekly meetings with Buddhist friends which led him to Throssel Hole, a Zen Buddhist monastery in the north east of England, where he became aware of the strong links between himself as a Christian and his Buddhist friends, and where he became aware of new dimensions of Christianity. He never felt that he would consider becoming a Buddhist in any serious way. He explained that learning and experiencing Buddhism was like learning another language. He could never make exact translations and there were some conflicting views, but some areas of faith which he had always found hard to articulate became clearer.

With these Buddhist friends, I was not becoming another person or denying my own faith, rather rejoicing to find the mystery of God celebrated in a way that opened me out to new possibilities within my own faith commitment. For example, I was learning about the importance of living by precepts of ethical training, and about 'just sitting', holding the turmoil of heart and mind in silent, loving awareness and letting that stillness expand into every activity of the day.[9]

Nicholas Allen's vocation to the religious life, through the Anglican Society of Saint Francis, grew while he was living and working among Buddhists in Korea, where becoming a monk or a nun seemed a natural development for many who followed a path of faith. When he returned to the UK he entered the religious life by testing his vocation as a friar, and as he did so he was inspired by a phrase from the Buddhist tradition, that he had gone 'from home to homelessness'. He wrote of his time in Korea and of:

The friends I made at the Lotus Lantern International Buddhist Centre where I attended meditation classes and study groups, and became for a while the librarian; conversations with monks at monasteries deep in the mountains; and so often, when walking in the mountains, coming across an isolated hermitage, the sound of the wind chime under the eaves and the scent of incense carrying my mind out into the vast openness of the mountain air.[10]

Early in 2003 I helped to run a ten-week course for Christians to listen to Hindus. The course was popular and the Christians who came to it did so to listen and learn, but they clearly found some of the Hindu expressions of their path of faith difficult to grasp. It was only as the course went on and as Christians and Hindus began to get to know each other that understanding and trust grew, not so much from what was said as from people's growing friendship and confidence in each other. Perhaps one of the most important evenings of the course was the one when dance and costume were introduced. Christians and Hindus alike dressed in beautiful Asian costumes and danced together.

One woman had initially introduced herself as an evangelical Christian who had almost decided not to come to the course. She forced herself to join in because she wanted to know more about the Hindu faith but as the course progressed she became very friendly with some of the Hindu people and the realization dawned on her that she had a lot in common with them and a lot to learn. She and the Hindu friends all approached their faith through routine daily religious practices, but above all they experienced God in all things and in all situations of life. Together they stand out from their surrounding culture.

Before the course ended the Hindu members asked the Christians to give a course to introduce Christianity to them. This was the first time the Christians in the group had been asked to do a presentation on their faith by members of another faith and they enjoyed sharing the preparation and the presentations enormously.

Following the listening courses I helped to arrange a discussion between youth leaders from the Christian and Hindu faiths. What emerged during the evening was revealing and challenging. The Hindu youth leader spoke with enthusiasm about the creativity of his work, which was enriching for him and for the young people, of whom there were hundreds. He spoke passionately about the weekly gatherings which are both spiritual and social. There is also the practical element of service to the community and especially to old people who are respected because they are spiritual. Old people are also the links between the past and the present, embodying the circle of life and death and life in themselves. The speaker explained that there are a few national occasions every year, usually in London or another large city, when hundreds of Hindu young people gather to listen to spiritual talks and to enjoy each other's company. Most of the Christians who listened to the talk were keen to go to a Hindu gathering of young people.

The Christian youth leader began his talk by expressing envy of the Hindu speaker. He said that even his own daughter was reluctant to say prayers at home, and, though she was still at primary school, she was beginning to complain about having to go to church. (His story reminded me of a friend whose daughter told her teachers and friends at school that her father was a window cleaner, because she was embarrassed to say that he was an Anglican bishop.) The Christian youth leader went on in his talk to explain how difficult it now is to gather young people together in many of the churches of Britain. He felt sad that he came from a church, the Methodist Church, that has a fine tradition of work with young people, including Sunday schools and youth clubs. The annual youth gathering in London used to be a highlight for young people, but sadly no longer happens.

There are young people in some of the churches of course and a few churches do have good activities for them. There are also very popular large gatherings, including Spring Harvest and the opportunities for young people to go to Taizé in Burgundy. One problem seems to be that, unlike what happens in the Hindu community, in the Christian community the connections between the special occasions and everyday life are often very tenuous and sometimes non-existent. Young people may return from Taizé to their local churches to find that no one is interested, and that there is no opportunity for them to share their experiences.

The discussion between Christian and Hindu youth leaders made it very clear that people of faith need each other and that young people are no exception. An inspiring event took place during the celebrations for the

Queen's Golden Jubilee, when eighty young people from all over the UK and from nine world faiths met in St James's Palace. Discussions were held on faith and service to the community. I met some of the young people and they were glowing through their new experiences, especially of meeting new friends of faiths different from their own. One of them later said:

> The Young People's Faith Forum was a good opportunity to meet people of different faiths, especially faiths that I'd only read about. It was interesting to listen to people of other faiths expressing their views and to deal with their perception of your own faith. I realized that although people of faiths have many things in common, this does not undermine or dilute each person's genuine commitment to their faith. You can be different but still be genuine and show real understanding and respect for others.[11]

No people have worked harder for recognition and understanding between people of the world faiths and for the development of the unity of believing and living than those of the Baha'i faith. The Baha'is teach that God has spoken to people through the world faiths, all having their particular insights and gifts to share. There are striking examples of this recognition in the houses of worship, one on each continent, where all people of all the faiths are welcome. The houses have nine sides, representing the nine world faiths. The scriptures of the world faiths are read and sung.

The Baha'i are challenged to turn to God and to live their lives in true piety and in service to others. Baha'is are taught to feed their souls by reading, prayer and meditation both at home and in the community. They are taught to open their hearts to others and to work positively for equality and justice between people. They are also encouraged to celebrate. The 19-day feast is an opportunity for the community to gather and to feel the links of fellowship and commitment which bind the members together and which also take them out into the world.

Baha'is read from the writings of their founder, Bahau'llah, every morning and every evening so that the words sink into their hearts and souls. Bahau'llah's life was one of vision, commitment and suffering. He was born into mid-nineteenth-century Persia and became part of the prophetic movement that grew from the teachings of the Bab (see p. 161). In 1852 he was put into a terrible dungeon in Tehran, where he realized that he was the person foretold by the Bab, chosen of God. In 1853 he and his family were expelled from Persia and never went back there. He moved around the Middle East, writing, preaching and spending periods of time in prison. He died in 1892 just outside the crusader city of Acre.

Bahau'llah taught about unity, the unity of God and of the human race in the world. A spiritual life is one which is lived in this faith and which seeks to put it into practice, in any circumstance or place, no matter how dire the situation or great the sacrifice. Bahau'llah was the latest in the line of great spiritual leaders who had known, taught and practised this simple yet extremely hard path towards holiness.

It is sometimes said that wholeness and holiness come to the people who are able to journey on through unhappiness and suffering without blaming other people or God. They rather use the experiences of suffering and struggle to learn more about themselves and about God, and to grow in love and service. Such people are therefore likely to be free of internal conflict and bitterness.

Someone who has suffered greatly and who has remained serenely involved with his people and with the wider world is the Dalai Lama. His suffering began when he was two years old, when he was taken away from his mother to undergo monastic training in Lhasa in Tibet. He was head of state when he was 15 and had to endure the invasion of Tibet by China, his own exile and the deaths of thousands of his people. Although many of the Tibetan people were welcomed in India, the Dalai Lama has never succeeded in his negotiations with China and they have never been able to return home to Tibet. His suffering continues as his own people criticize him for his many failures of diplomacy and as they feel the pain of Tibet and their culture and faith being slowly but surely destroyed.

The wonder is that the Dalai Lama is a serene person who communicates generously, often smiling and always sensitive to others. I have heard him speak with love and optimism twice and I have met him once, when, for a second or two, I was astonished by his peaceful and kindly attention.

It is sometimes said that human inability to experience wholeness of life, true holiness, is due to too much striving by working hard to change things, rather than by working more naturally and through faith, real situations and people. Working through life, with God, may lead to the experience or conviction that, no matter how terrible or even trivial life may seem, it is somehow leading somewhere, and that no matter how small or trivial an act of grace and love may be, it is nevertheless a contribution towards wholeness and holiness. Edith Sitwell's famous phrase in her poem 'Eurydice' was written in relation to death, but is equally relevant in relation to life: 'All in the end is harvest.'

Joel Elkes is someone who understands and lives his spiritual journey with its many joys and woes, successes and failures. Joel and his sister Sara lost their famous father Dr Elchanan Elkes in Dachau concentration camp in World War Two. They are sad but not bitter, and above all they are proud that their father remained a real person of faith and love in spite of all his sufferings. They are proud that their father died because, as a medical officer, he refused to name those who were too weak to work in the camp and himself went on hunger strike in protest. Joel gave a lecture on his father's life and death. He asked people always to remember the Holocaust: '[T]he story of the Holocaust must be taught, not only as a stark and terrible warning for our dangerous times, but as an affirmation of our humanity and of hope.'[12] Hope never left Dr. Elkes, and it has never left his son and daughter. They see a wholeness and holiness in the life of their father, who 'was never in doubt about his values, and never for one moment lost his belief in his people'.[13]

Joel Elkes has always lived his own life to the full. He is a distinguished Jewish professor who has pioneered research into the play of chemical influences on mental life and who has founded programmes of behavioural medicine. He has written recently about the importance of awareness of the link between the ordinary things in life and the mysterious dimensions many people experience. He said, 'One of the greatest pleasures I know comes from staring at objects, and listening into a conversation between the mundane and the mysterious.' He paints using watercolours so that every painting grows naturally and unpredictably, with a life of its own. 'Mistakes, once made, endure: like life itself one learns to live with them.'

The Jewish festival of Sukkot, the feast of tabernacles or dwelling in booths, is a festival of people who have learnt to live life with God through all their troubles and joys over many centuries of persecution and loss, courage and support for each other. The festival takes place five days after the Day of Atonement and lasts for nine days.

During this festival every family builds and decorates a booth with the boughs of leafy trees and the 'fruit of a goodly tree'. The fruit is the citron. There are also the palm branches, the myrtle and the willow. The people eat all their meals in the booths and sometimes sleep there.

The booths are a reminder to the people of the time when they lived in tents in the wilderness for 40 years with

God watching over them. They are a link to the Jewish community around the world and through history to a time of suffering and hope which has brought them to where they are today. The festival of Sukkot, like all the festivals, is both a spiritual experience and the glue that holds the family and the community together in wholeness; and in reaching out, through learning and good deeds, for holiness.

Loren Eisley, the anthropologist, told a story from a time when he was exploring on a beach in Mexico. He saw a man bending down on the edge of the sea, picking something up and tossing it into the waves. Eisley realized that he was picking up starfish and tossing them into the sea. He spoke to the man, pointing out that tossing a few starfish into the sea was ridiculous because there are thousands of miles of beach and millions of starfish. Saving a few starfish could make no difference at all. The response of the starfish thrower was to pick up another starfish and to throw it into the waves, saying, 'It makes a difference to this one.'

People of faith are challenged to become starfish throwers, having the faith to live by making their contribution of love, no matter how small or seemingly trivial it may be, thus growing in wholeness and holiness and thus also making a difference.

Some challenging words from the poet Saadi from Shiraz are woven into the carpet in the United Nations building in New York:

All people are members of the same body

Created from one essence
If fate brings suffering to one member
The others cannot stay at rest.
You who remain indifferent to the burden of pain of others
Do not deserve to be called human.

People who live in faith are above all human, living in the real world of joy and woe in a way that relieves suffering and enhances the living and loving of others. They are bridge-builders towards the possibility of wholeness and holiness for us all.

3

Witnessing to faith

Friends from South India tell the story of a village now called Nazareth in the diocese of Tirunelveli in the Church of South India. About a hundred years ago the Hindu village was visited by Christian missionaries who cared for the people and shared their faith. After some time the whole village became Christian with the new name 'Nazareth', a church was built and the Hindu temple was burnt down. Nazareth has been Christian ever since.

Recently in Rwanda in Central Africa some people have been moving in another direction, towards Islam. More than ten years after the genocide in Rwanda, when about a million people were slaughtered, those who survived are reflecting on what happened to them and some have said that, though Rwanda was a Christian country, it was the few Muslims who were there who helped them in their time of crisis and even saved their lives. Some of those who were saved have moved from Christianity to Islam.

An Englishman who grew up with no faith at all, in a family which was avowedly atheistic, always felt that there was something missing from his life and gradually came to realize that he lacked and longed for a spiritual dimension. He met members of the Sikh community in India, England and America and at last made the decision to become a Sikh. He chose to join the Sikh faith because it includes so many of the values he grew up with, including love of the community and service and respect for others.

A woman from the Caribbean who lived in the Midlands felt somehow uneasy as a member of the Christian faith. She was introduced to the Baha'i faith by a friend and read from the teachings of Bahau'llah. She was very moved by the readings and a few months later she became a Baha'i. She has been a Baha'i for more than ten years now. She feels completely at home and is especially keen to share her faith's teachings about justice, unity and love.

If we are Christians reading these stories of movement from one faith to another we will not have the same reaction to them. While people of other faiths will also have mixed reactions to the stories, it seems that Christians disagree with each other most about the urgency or not for Christians to witness to people of other faiths and about conversion between the faiths. There is a whole range of Christian views of other faiths, and these differing views are likely to determine the approach concerning, dialogue, witness and conversion.[1]

I have approached this chapter as someone who has many friends who are members of the world faiths, both in the UK and around the world. I trust my friends and enjoy my work with them, work from which I and many others learn. As friendship grows it is my experience that we may learn more, not only about the other faiths, but, equally importantly, about our own. I have not moved from this experience to take up a theological view in relation to the other faiths because I have not found it helpful or possible to do so. I am not a pilgrim in another faith tradition and, rather, learn about the other faiths through their pilgrims, those who stand in their traditions and who follow their paths of faith, the paths they believe to be best for them. I read about the other faiths and visit their places of worship and community. I experience many people of other faiths as true pilgrims whose lives are uplifting to myself and to others.

I have not asked whether the pilgrims of other faiths are saved but neither would I ask this question of another Christian. I believe that Jesus the Christ is part of the Godhead all people will ultimately see (John 14.6). It does not however follow that all people must claim Jesus while they are alive on the Earth.

It is obvious that not all Christians share my position or experience. Very often the theological traditions of Christian groups determine the sympathy or lack of it with which other faiths and their members are regarded. The approach to witness and evangelism also varies. However, the groups are not firm and fixed; they have blurred edges, there are many overlaps and grey areas and they are only useful as a rough guide, an aid to the beginning of understanding. People may fit into more than one group and many are likely to move between at least two of the groups as their experience and thinking develop.

Some Christians state that they cannot understand the other faiths at all. They recognize that the other faiths have grown up in different contexts and in response perhaps to different questions. They accept that the other faiths exist but can see no relationship between them and perhaps no point in trying to create one. They do not make judgements, and are content to live and let live.

There are Christians who believe that salvation can only be attained through an affirmation of Jesus Christ, and since Jesus is the centre of the Christian faith, and of no other faith, all other faiths must be rejected and their members, if possible, converted to Christianity for the good of their eternal souls. Those holding this view see the Bible as the highest authority, the one absolute source of knowledge about God and about people. They proclaim Jesus as the only saviour of the world and the need for every person to have experience of his saving power. They also emphasize the necessity of evangelism, of witnessing about the faith to every person, with the hope and prayer that all will come to salvation through becoming Christian.

The need for Jewish people to become Christian is at the heart of Christian Zionism, for example. Christian Zionists support the return of the Jews to the land of Israel, their 'promised land', but also see it as essential that the same Jews convert to Christianity.

Many Christians point out that Christianity has always been a missionary faith, from the time when Jesus proclaimed the 'Good News', died on the cross and rose from the dead. Members of the early Church took great risks to witness, many giving their lives, then and throughout history. The 'great commission' challenged and continues to challenge Christians to: 'Go therefore and make disciples of all nations, baptizing them in the name of the Father and of the Son and of the Holy Spirit' (Matthew 28.18-20).

Some members of the 'exclusive' group of Christians, and they are growing in numbers, accept that study of other faiths and dialogue with people of other faiths is necessary because it is necessary to understand people before trying to convert them.

This, of course, can lead to unforeseen consequences. A study of Christian missions in nineteenth-century Sri Lanka indicates that missionary activity and involvement in understanding other faiths and cultures may divide missionaries into those who become increasingly more sympathetic to the faith of those they are hoping to convert, and those who become less sympathetic as they engage with that same faith. There were, it seems, more missionaries in the negative group, who saw the Buddhism they encountered as nihilistic, atheistic and largely morally impotent.[2] The mistrust of some has continued to this day, so that when Pope John Paul II visited Sri Lanka in 1995 many Buddhists protested. This protest was partly against Pope John Paul's book *Crossing the Threshold of Hope*, in which he portrayed Buddhism negatively.

However, the encounter with Buddhism and with Buddhists in Sri Lanka did lead some Christians to an appreciation and respect which led them to move further on to learn Pali and to develop firm friendships. Dialogue and friendship have continued among many groups into the twentieth and twenty-first centuries. A good example in Sri Lanka is the work of Devasarana, founded by Yohan

Devananda in a rural area near to Kurunagela. It is a centre that has moved from dialogue between the faiths to the faiths working together for grassroots development for peasants. A new and exciting twenty-first-century development is the beginning of a women's religious community for women of all the faiths of Sri Lanka, Buddhist, Hindu, Christian and Muslim.

This experience of positions changing as another faith is engaged with is not unique to Christians in Sri Lanka. Someone who has been called the greatest twentieth-century Christian missioner, Max Warren, is also someone who, as a result of his encounter with people of other faiths and his study of the faiths themselves, moved his position more than once.[3] As his thinking and experience developed, influenced by Temple Gairdner of Cairo and Kenneth Cragg, he became anxious to display his friendship for people of other faiths and to offer a model of ministry that was open and respectful of others while at the same time remaining true to his evangelical roots and honest wish for conversions to Christianity. In his introduction to one volume in the Christian Presence series, Kenneth Cragg's *Sandals at the Mosque*, published in 1959, he wrote what has become a famous statement:

When we approach the man of another faith than our own it will be in a spirit of expectancy to find how God has been speaking to him and what new understandings of the grace and love of God we may ourselves discover in this encounter.

Our first task in approaching another people, another culture, another religion, is to take off our shoes, for the place we are approaching is holy. Else we may find ourselves treading on men's dreams. More serious still, we may forget that God was here before our arrival.[4]

Max Warren gradually moved in his thinking and writing to begin to refer to the Cosmic Christ being there in the whole universe, including the beliefs and traditions of other religions. He spoke of meeting the Christ when he met someone of another faith and he emphasized the need for mutual listening and learning.

Max Warren's model for mission became the simple and powerful one of being there with people, loving them, learning their culture, language and ways and thus, informally and naturally, representing the Christ and his love for all.

Now, of course, this movement in a faith position can be regarded very differently by different Christians. One might see a movement like that of Max Warren as a development in depth, understanding and maturity in faith. Another might see the same development as a loss of Christian clarity, or even a betrayal of the uniqueness of Christ, and so a loss of way.

My position and experience is very much the former of these. For me, being there with people requires time, but more important than time is an attitude of openness to the reality of the others, their lives and struggles, hopes and dreams. Mutual openness arising from relationships of respect and love may lead to new dimensions of understanding and a new way forward in being Church.

I have spent many summers in Kenya, working with Christians there on various projects, including tree planting, building and water engineering. Godfrey Ngungire Wanjohi is a friend who has managed to become an important link person between his own Kikuyu people and the Maasai people: he is someone who works and feels at home with the Maasai, understanding their culture, hopes, dreams and troubles. He lives with his family in Kagongo near Othaya, on the edge of the Abedare Mountains, and travels regularly to the Maasai lands beyond the town of Dol Dol, where he meets the people, discusses issues and problems they are facing, and buys the honey they have collected and refined. The honey is sold to the Kikuyu people and the money earned is used by the Maasai to supplement their diet and to send the children to school. The simple act of being there and of buying the honey has given both the Kikuyu Christians and the Maasai people a new respect for each other. There have been divisions and even animosities in the past, largely due to the two tribes stereotyping each other. This is now less likely. There is openness and listening and a new determination by both peoples to work together.

Joseph Ranja Ole Mepukori is the parish priest for a huge area of semi-desert in the Maasai lands visited by Godfrey. Joseph walks in search of the people, setting off from his small family homestead very early in the morning and not returning until midnight or often a few days later. He moves naturally from one nomadic group to another, asking the first people he meets where others may be found. He shares issues of schooling for the children, water supplies and the state of the cattle and goats. He is a natural witness to his Christian faith with his Maasai friends, most of whom retain their traditional religion. One of his ways of 'being there' is to listen to the stories of the people: he has made a collection of stories and traditional prayers. He sometimes uses the stories and prayers in the church services, thus honouring both the traditionalists and the Maasai who have come into the church as practising Christians.

One of the traditional Maasai prayers now used in Christian services in Kenya may bring home to Christians the awe with which the one God is held in the traditional Maasai religion:

Almighty and powerful God,
God of the Ancestors,
The black God who is the God of peace,
I come out having nothing,
Being naked,
waiting for you, O God to clothe me.

I am blessed, and you are the one who has blessed
    me.
You satisfy me with blessed gifts that come from
    you,
as you promised.
I will wait the fulfilment from you, O God,
because you said so.[5]

No one better represents the missionary model of being
there than Ronald Wynne, who went to live with the
Hambukushu people of Botswana for many years. The
Hambukushu people were refugees from Angola and for
six years Ronald Wynne simply lived with them, learning
the language and the history and culture of the people. As
he shared their experiences of being refugees he gradually
told stories of the Hebrew people who were refugees. Later
he told stories of Jesus of Nazareth. What emerged, after
many years, was a new and African church, but it emerged
because the people wanted it and created it as part of their
community and culture.

A friend of Max Warren, who became closer as
Warren's own thought developed, was Raymundo
Panniker, a Roman Catholic priest who had a Spanish
Roman Catholic mother and a Hindu father. He grew to
believe that no member of a religion can enter a real
relationship with a member of another religion in the
belief that their own religion is the norm. He has
developed an understanding of the 'universal Christ', who
is the 'totality of reality', the link between all that is,
beginning and ending, earthly and heavenly. He
understands the Cosmic Christ as being incarnated in
Jesus of Nazareth but has gone on to explain that this does
not mean that the incarnation of the Christ is limited to
the Jesus of history. He suggests that, though Jesus is the
Christ, the Christ is much more than Jesus.

The Roman Catholic Church largely accepted that there
is a partial truth in the other world faiths after the Second

Vatican Council. The Council's 'Declaration on the Relation of the Church to Non-Christian Religions' states:

> Throughout history even to the present day, there is found among different peoples a certain awareness of a hidden power, which lies behind the course of nature and the events of human life. At times there is present even a recognition of a supreme being, or still more of a Father ... The Catholic Church rejects nothing of what is true and holy in these religions. She has a high regard for the manner of life, their precepts and doctrines which ... often reflect a ray of that truth which enlightens all men. Yet she proclaims and is in duty bound to proclaim without fail, Christ who is the way, the truth and the life. In him, in whom God reconciled all things to himself, men find the fullness of their religious life.[6]

Roman Catholics recognize that God, who was revealed in Jesus, was also revealed through other faiths than Christianity. They point to the Old and New Testaments, where there is the recognition of God with other peoples. Pope Paul VI set up the Pontifical Council for Inter-Religious Dialogue and this continues to receive the full support of the Vatican. In 1986 there was a gathering of the leaders of the world faiths in Assisi. They were invited by the Pope to what is now remembered as a symbol of the commitment of the Church to dialogue and friendship between people of the world faiths.

Roman Catholics also emphasize that the Holy Spirit has an existence that includes the whole of creation. As a church, however, they do not feel that other faiths than the Christian faith can lead people into full truth, for they believe that it is only through knowing and loving Jesus the Christ that it is possible to fully know and to love God, and to be saved.

Mother Theresa of Calcutta fits into this group. She longed for people to be Christian but spoke of being inspired to do the work she did, in caring for the poor and downtrodden all around her, by seeing the face of God in them. She was not worn out by her labours because the poor people themselves, the Hindu and Muslim people in the streets of Calcutta, pointed her to God. Their devout patience reminded her that God was with them. She was thus given the energy she needed to carry on, a devout Christian serving others in a very practical and down-to-earth way.

Many thinkers have accepted the Christ as the one saviour of the world, without whom there would be no possibility of people in the world knowing and responding to God, but have felt, like Raymundo Panniker, that knowledge and acceptance of the Christ are not necessary because the Christ event has permeated the whole of creation and the whole of history. Christians are therefore called upon to learn to recognize the presence and work of Christ who does not belong to one religion but is in all of them.

The World Council of Churches (WCC) struggled with its programme for dialogue with people of other faiths which began in 1971, with many people continuing to see the great commission as urgent and central to Christian responsibility. In 1990 the WCC launched a four-year programme of study, 'My Neighbour's Faith and Mine – Theological Discoveries Through Inter Faith Dialogue'. Members of the Roman Catholic, Orthodox and Protestant Churches took part in the study and reached agreement that it was not possible for a God of love, compassion and grace, the God Christians know and love through Jesus the Christ, to have withdrawn from his own creation simply because it had not become Christian. The meetings took place in Baar near Zurich. The Baar Declaration affirmed the many religious traditions as being part of God's providence and stated that, where there is 'wisdom, insight, knowledge, understanding, love and holiness', they are the gifts of the Holy Spirit.[7]

Those who made the Baar Declaration understood, with most Christians, that the great commission will always be there, and that it will always be a challenge, but it is no longer an urgent or harsh challenge. It continues to be important for Christians to go to all nations and to share the good news of Christ, but it may be a sharing that is gentle, relaxed and through friendship, a sharing with those with whom the Christ is already present, who make their own ongoing decisions about their faiths and lives and who have much also to share.

Aloysius Pieris is a Sri Lankan Jesuit who has written about his experience of finding the Christ at the heart of the Asian religions, including the Buddhist faith and culture of his country. He has spoken very critically of Christians who try to take on something of Asian culture but who do not appreciate Asian religion. They are not therefore prepared to change in any way, but are rather adding an extra layer of culture. He challenges Christians to enter Asian religion for its own sake, as a place where they may learn and grow and change. When I visited Tulana, his study centre in Sri Lanka, he told the story of his own journey into Hinduism, when he travelled through India. When he was on the banks of the Ganges, where he was surrounded by Hindu people who were praying and making offerings, he was so taken up by the atmosphere around him that he was overcome by a longing for God and, for him, the most appropriate way to respond to this longing was, surrounded by the worshipping Hindus, to celebrate a Mass.

Henri Le Saux was a French Benedictine monk who was better known as Swami Abhishiktananda. He went to India in 1948, lived in Shantivanam ashram and then moved to the Himalayas where he lived as a hermit and died in 1973. He lived his understanding that God is in all the world, its faiths and peoples. He saw the Christian approach to others as one of service and sharing amongst equals. He immersed himself in Hinduism so much that

Hindu spirituality was his spirituality. In his *Hindu–Christian Meeting Point* he wrote of the awakening of the Church to Christ in the other faiths:

> With reverent wonder she finds that in the hearts of those to whom the name of the Lord is still unknown his Spirit is already at work, bringing them to fulfillment and resurrection. She sees that this is not in spite of, but precisely through the instrumentality of their various religious traditions, their rituals and Scriptures, and the spiritual vigour and thirst for renunciation which these have transmitted from generation to generation.[8]

Some Christians are unhappy with the idea that people of other faiths are seen by other Christians, however respectfully and lovingly, in relation to their own Christian faith. If one is a member of another faith then the idea of the Cosmic Christ and the hidden Christ may be experienced as an attempt to take over and incorporate the other religions into Christianity. This group of Christians suggests that a loving God, who was shown through Jesus as accepting a wide variety of people, would not be revealed in other faiths than the Christian faith without also offering complete independence including the possibility of salvation through the other faiths. One of the pioneers of this group is John Hick, who moved from an evangelical position to introduce what he called a Copernican revolution in theology. This revolution was from a Jesus-centred to a God-centred model of the world faiths. The revolution makes it possible to see the world faiths, including Christianity, as human responses to the reality of the one God, which have developed in different historical, geographical and cultural settings.

This view might accept the main world faiths as equal but does not accept all religious expression as equal. Hick has suggested that it is important to ask whether or not a religious belief makes it possible for its followers to move from being self-centred to being centred on 'reality' and thus committed to work for justice in the world.

The call is for members of all faiths to seek truth together as equals and to work for justice in the world through the activity of the Holy Spirit, at work in the world and never confined to the Church. There is perhaps common ground here between Christians in many groups who approach the other world faiths and their pilgrims with honesty, respect and love. The fruits of the Spirit are the opposite of self-centred selfishness: love, joy, peace, patience, kindness, goodness, trustfulness, gentleness and self control (Galatians 5.22).

The fruits of the Spirit are obviously not confined to Christians but are also evident in people of other cultures and faiths, one of the most obvious twentieth-century examples being Mahatma Gandhi. Gandhi was a Hindu who gave his life to work for the freedom of his country from the British and at the same time for a recognition of the dignity and worth of the poorest people of India, those he called 'Children of God'. Gandhi understood the Sermon on the Mount as the essence of the teaching of Jesus Christ. The sermon and the *Bhagavad Gita* were the inspiration by which Gandhi lived. He saw Jesus as the perfect man, who dies and is resurrected from day to day. He saw no need to consider becoming a Christian because he believed that he should be a good Hindu and thus be close to the Christ. He pointed out that it is not the person who says 'Lord, Lord' who is a Christian, but rather he who does the will of the Lord.

The need for understanding, peace, and justice in the early twenty-first-century world is so great and also so much at the heart of the idea of the Kingdom of God that some would say that people of faith should no longer be put into categories according to their faiths but rather through their attitudes and actions. People of faith who take up stances of separation, superiority or intolerance towards people of other faiths may fit into John Hick's self-centred group and may need to be challenged to move towards shared work for justice with those who are working in the same direction in the other world faiths. Chapter 5, 'Only one world', explores some of the encouraging work being done by people of faith working together for a peaceful and just world.

If we are to live within our own faith and also to be at ease with the faiths of others it becomes necessary for us to appreciate the others, whether we wish them to become Christian or not. Hopefully we may also be able to recognize that others, like Mahatma Gandhi, are where they are in faith because they know it as the place for them to be, and, further, that we might learn from them.[9] If we are able to come to this position we are also liberated to share our faith, realizing that conversion can only come from within the person who is converted, through the love of God, and not from the will of someone else.

A friend who has since died told me his story of becoming a Christian from a Zoroastrian upbringing.[10] This story is noteworthy because it shows a natural movement from one faith to another, simply because it was the right thing to do for the person who moved.

Nadir Dinshaw was born into a Zoroastrian family in Karachi in 1925 and grew up to love his faith, with its focus on good thoughts, good words and good deeds. He said that he was especially admiring of King Cyrus who freed the Jews from the Babylonian captivity in 539 BCE. Cyrus made no attempt to impose his Zoroastrian faith on the Jewish people, but rather encouraged all his subjects to live a good life. He allowed the Jews to rebuild the temple in Jerusalem.

Nadir was most influenced by his Zoroastrian grandmother, whom he described as a loving and selfless saint. 'She loved laughter and cheerfulness, and the poor, and people of all kinds, even the most unlovable. Above all, she loved giving.'[11] Nadir's grandmother seems, through what she was as a practising Zoroastrian, to have pointed him towards Christianity. He became a Christian in his mid-thirties, his love for his grandmother being taken up and joined to his love for Jesus and Mary, whom he discerned as having the same qualities as his grandmother, and in complete perfection. He said the Magnificat every night of his life after he became a Christian and always strove to serve the poor and suffering. The people he admired were philanthropists who were committed to their faith but always open to people of other faiths. He was deeply influenced by Bishop Christopher Robinson of the Delhi Brotherhood of the Ascended Christ, who taught him to see God in the poor Hindu and Muslim people of India, and taught him further to see the qualities of the Kingdom of God in people of other faiths as well as in Christians:

> Remember, Nadir, there is no such thing as a particularly Christian virtue; all the great virtues are universal; and no faith can claim a monopoly of them; there are Christ-like virtues, but those are usually to be found more often in non-Christians than in Christians.[12]

Nadir became a Christian but he did so without rejecting Zoroastrianism. He said that both religions were a part of him. He said that the feast of the Epiphany was always a very special time, when the journey of the Magi, the Zoroastrian sages, from Persia to Bethlehem, is remembered. He always felt that the journey brought together the two religions, his two faith families.

Nadir was always happy to share the story of how he became a Christian with others. It is a good model for the sharing of faith, because it is loving and gentle. It is consistent with the faith itself, which must be shared, as it has been shared from the time of the first Christians. The sharing of faith in openness and love is the way in which the Church remains the Church rather than a sect or a club, and the same may be said of any of the world faiths.

Islam is, like Christianity, a missionary religion. Muslims firmly believe that their faith and its message are for the whole of humanity. Most Muslims have been devastated by their post-9/11 reputation for violence and many are working hard to help people to see them as true people of faith. One example, in August 2004, is a project that has come from one of the north London Muslim communities, to send videos, DVDs and books about Islam to many of the public libraries in the UK. Most Muslims have become even more anxious since the London bombings of 7 July 2005, and many are trying to make contact and develop friendship with people of other faiths in their localities.

The Lord Buddha is known to have joined in preaching journeys. He also challenged his disciples to share his message as widely as possible. The sharing has been successful in that Buddhism has spread from its beginnings in Hinduism in northern India to Sri Lanka, Burma, Thailand, Cambodia and Vietnam, China, Japan and Korea. Other founders of eastern religions also hoped that their insights and teachings would be shared.

We, many of the people of all faiths, hope that people of other faiths than our own will join us, but if we are wise we will not have a plan for this to happen and will be relaxed, leaving the outcome to God with the other person or people.

Dialogue and friendship lead naturally to witness; they do not replace it. If dialogue is genuine, and not simply the superficial politeness that can prevail at some formal interfaith gatherings, then sooner or later, as trust develops, issues of faith, and burning issues associated with faith, must come to the surface and be shared. This has always been the case in groups I have belonged to and, though it can initially lead to some difficulties, it is always refreshing. The feeling of things being hidden and of relationships being partial disappears.

Perhaps this variety of experience from differing faith traditions can be summed up in the Jewish saying 'God gave each of us two ears but only one mouth so that we can listen carefully before speaking.'

When faith is shared at a deep level by people of more than one faith it becomes immediately obvious that the faiths are not alike, but very different from each other. By this time the participants have grown to trust each other and to enjoy each other's company. The problem of the differences between the faiths has then to be overcome and this can only be done by continued trust that friends of other faiths are where it is right for them to be and by simple acceptance of the authenticity of their journey. This is only possible if participants in the sharing are relaxed, and make the conscious decision to listen as well as to speak, to learn as well as to share. As has already been said, listening is not easy for people of any faith, since we have all grown up and remained in our faith because we have experienced it as wonderful, inspiring, truth.

I remember the moment in an interfaith group when a good Muslim friend said that Muslims do not accept the crucifixion and resurrection of Jesus. The Christians in the room were at first embarrassed and unsure of how to respond and then some of them affirmed that they did believe in the crucifixion and resurrection of Jesus who is the Christ. The Muslim friend said that he knew this, that it was good to know where we differ and then to accept the difference. He said, 'We are never going to agree about this, even if we talk all day, all night and for ever. We have to put it on one side and share some of the beliefs and commitments to action we do have in common.'

A similar decision was made by a group of Christian and Jewish people who met over a period of ten years, when they came to discuss Israel's position as the promised land of the Jewish people. They decided that it was important to share different views, but then to accept that they were all different, rather than to go on discussing, with the danger of the discussion becoming a quarrel.[13] They remained a relaxed group of very good friends, who could work together.

The sharing of faith which is not relaxed can be experienced by others as aggressive and even threatening. A Buddhist friend told of a Christian who had tried to convert him by talking all the time about Christianity in a very enthusiastic way, but never listening to the Buddhist response. The attitude of the 'evangelist' was that it was quite obvious that the Buddhist should become a Christian, with no thought of what Buddhism meant to him. Such narrowly focused and single-minded witness is not only unhelpful but also inhuman. The 'evangelist' has cut herself off from the real world to such an extent that she is no longer able to listen to other people, even to Christians who are less zealous in their approach to others.

The story of the conquest of Peru is, like many stories of conquest, one of military victory followed by oppressive cultural and religious domination. The conquered Inca Atahualpa would not become a Christian, no matter how hard the Franciscan missionary tried to persuade him. Argument gave way to torture, but still the Inca refused to give in and become a Christian. The threat of execution prompted the Inca to find out more and he asked whether, if he became a Christian, he would go to heaven and meet other Christians. The affirmative answer gave him the strength to die as he had lived, as an Inca, for his experience meant that he never wanted to meet another Christian, in life or after death.

There are, sadly, many bad examples of Christian mission, when the missionaries went out to convert, with little or no respect for the way of life or even the religion of those they met. It is not surprising that Christianity, or any other religion, which is presented in an aggressive, narrow or self-righteous way, which judges those who are of a different faith as unworthy of being listened to, is not attractive.

In Zadie Smith's novel *White Teeth*, Samad Iqbal, who lives in north-west London, longs for one of his two sons to be a devout Muslim, uncontaminated by worldly and especially by western influences. So he sends Majid, his 'clever' son, to be brought up in Bangladesh. He thinks that by doing this he will ensure that Majid will be the good traditional Muslim he can be proud of in his old age. He is bitterly disappointed when Majid returns to England as a well-educated and questioning student, a lover of maths and science and an agnostic towards all religion.[14]

Francis Xavier was a sixteenth-century missionary who set off from Portugal for India with a very narrow attitude to those he hoped to convert. He is interesting because he changed his attitude as he went along, and, although he always wished to convert the people he met, he did learn to respect them and he did gradually understand the need to learn about and to share with them. At first he spoke of creating a 'blank sheet' by destroying all signs of 'idolatry' before imposing Christianity. He baptized thousands of people in South India before leaving for Japan, where he landed in 1549. Once in Japan he changed because it was obvious to him that unless he did so he would not be listened to. He learnt the language of the people so that he could discuss religion with them, and he wore Japanese dress. He began to speak of mission as long-term rather than a conquest.

The Portuguese missionaries in India at first adopted the 'clean sheet' model of mission, but a more hopeful model was adopted by the Jesuit Robert de Nobili who arrived in South India in 1605. His way of working with the people as one of them is the pattern that has mostly been followed by the Jesuits and some others in India since then. He wore the yellow robes and clogs of the Brahmin caste and put on the sacred thread. He learnt Tamil and Sanskrit and studied Indian philosophy. He even, very controversially, adapted to the Hindu caste system by establishing a new category of missionaries to minister to the lower castes, and he encouraged Christians to take part in some Hindu festivals.

The witness of Robert de Nobili in India focused on a gentle and loving way of working with the people of another faith who were all around him. P. Chenchiah was perhaps a twentieth-century descendent of Robert de Nobili. He was a lawyer who came from a Brahmin family. He hoped that Christianity, a natural partner with Hinduism, would make the Christ evident in human lives. He said:

> The convert of today regards Hinduism as his spiritual mother, who has nurtured him in a sense of spiritual values of the past. He discovers the supreme value of Christ, not in spite of Hinduism, but because Hinduism has taught him to discern spiritual greatness. For him loyalty to Christ does not involve the surrender of a reverential attitude towards the Hindu heritage.[15]

Interfaith dialogue, in which witness to faith is central, is not an option for people of faith, but, rather, an essential part of their lives. When faiths are shared honestly and openly, when there is true listening, all those involved have the freedom to change. This may mean that the person of faith is offered a new insight into his or her own faith from the different faith of another person. Witness is a crucial element of Christianity, but it must be conducted in the spirit of the faith itself to be valid. God loved and loves the world and all its people and not just those who are members of the Church.

We know that in his meetings with other people Jesus always gave those he met the freedom to respond or not. The Samaritan people were not acceptable to the Jewish people, but Jesus moved among them, spoke to them and developed relationships with them in which he as well as they learnt. He told the story of the Good Samaritan, the one true person who gave help to the man in need by the roadside (Luke 10.29–37). He held a conversation, or dialogue, with the Canaanite woman during which he listened and changed. When the woman pointed out that even dogs eat the food left under their master's table, Jesus came to realize that he was making false distinctions between Jews and Gentiles (Matthew 15.22–28).

It is now many years since Vincent Donovan lived with the Maasai people in Tanzania. As he shared his Christian faith with them he realized that he had made false distinctions between himself and them, for all were people of God. He wrote about his experiences.[16] A significant moment occurred when a Maasai chief asked Donovan whether his Christian God loved the Christians more than he loved the Maasai. He went on to say that if he did love the Christians more then he must be a tribal God. The answer was obvious to Vincent Donovan. He came to know and love the Maasai people as a people loved by God, whether they were Christian or not. He shared his Christian faith with them because it was an essential part of him, and because he believed that knowing Christ would enrich their lives. He himself was enriched by his friendship with the Maasai and through what he learnt from them.

Verrier Elwin was an Anglican priest who worked as a missionary in India before moving away from the Church to 'follow the Crucified among the crucified'. He went to live with the tribal people in north-eastern India, identifying with them and serving them. He was born in 1902, went to India in 1927 and stayed there until his death in 1964. He went to India to serve the suffering people and it was they who gave him the title of 'Din-Sevak' which means 'servant of the poor'.[17]

Religious mission to poor people is often treated with suspicion. Some say that such mission is easy because the poor benefit from the worldly advantages the missionaries bring, including education and health care, and that it would therefore be strange or even foolish if they refused the new religion. This criticism brings out very clearly why it is vital that people are not bribed with education and food, but are treated with respect and left free to make their own decisions. Christians understand from the Gospels that Jesus saw his ministry as 'good news to the poor', but he never patronized those he met and worked with, always approaching them with respect.

There is the story of a time when Jesus travelled along the border between Samaria and Galilee. He began to go into one of the villages when ten men who were suffering from the dreaded skin disease of leprosy shouted at him from the distance, because they dared not approach someone who was not also suffering. Jesus stopped in his tracks and they asked him to offer them pity. Jesus told them to go to the priests for examination but when they were on the way there they suddenly realized that the disease had disappeared. One of the men, a Samaritan, immediately turned back, to praise God and to thank Jesus for healing him. Jesus naturally asked, 'There were ten men who were healed; where are the other nine?' (Luke 12.11–17)

Witnessing to faith is not an exercise of taking the truth out to the world, but rather of sharing insights and experiences in a world where God is already present and with people who are loved by God. This witnessing to faith is not an arduous task, where the 'evangelist' is doing everything, but, rather, a life-bringing experience for those who take part and who recognize its value and wish to be part of it, who are all learning together and working together. And seen in this way no part of the world is hostile, but a place of learning and of partnership for all those of goodwill who recognize the good things of God. Further, there are no people Christians cannot work with, whether of other faiths or of no faith, so long as they are fellow pilgrims in seeking and working for the qualities of the Kingdom of God. If they are not such pilgrims they will freely excuse themselves, but until they do so they cannot be identified. There are always surprises.

In summary, then, Christians and people of other faiths can be a mutual blessing if we trust and accept one another as gifts from God.

The book of Genesis includes the story of the mysterious king/priest called Melchizedek who came and went from the stage of history by giving Abram bread and wine and blessing him, before the covenant between God and Abram (later Abraham) had been made, before, therefore, the Jewish faith had been born. Abram responded by giving Melchizedek one tenth of everything, thus recognizing him as a true priest/king, a representative of God – an encounter of mutual blessing which the author of the Epistle to the Hebrews develops as prefiguring the eternal priesthood of Jesus the Christ.

I recently had my own 'Melchizedek experience'. I was involved in a road accident, when a tyre bursting on another car caused it to fly across the motorway into the back of my car. I went round and round in the road, finally coming to a halt on the central reservation, facing the wrong way with traffic shooting past me. I was dazed but thankfully unharmed. Before anyone else arrived, a car stopped beside me and the driver asked if he could do anything to help. I had hardly said 'Yes' when the police and ambulance arrived and a coach also pulled up. The driver of the car waited, while all the forms were filled in and the checks made. He took my luggage into his car and offered to drive me to wherever I wanted to go, which was not where he was going. I gratefully accepted and was driven to my destination, several hours after the accident had taken place. When I thanked the driver of the car he said, 'Why are we here on Earth unless it is to help each other?' When I asked if he was a member of a faith he told me that he was a Muslim. Then this stranger, this modern-day Melchizedek, having blessed me in my hour of need, went on his way. What witness to faith could be more powerful?

4

Divisions, suffering and strife

> How many evils has religion caused!
>
> Lucretius

The dance of the Hindu god Shiva is one of the world's most powerful symbols of faith in action. Shiva, wearing a belt of austerity, and surrounded by a ring of fire, is poised with his knee raised in a dance of creation and of destruction. His foot is placed on a creature representing the evil forces of the world and his hand is pointing downwards in commitment to the world and its people.

Shiva's dance challenges all people of faith to be not amongst the forces of evil but to work for a world where justice will prevail. If even half the people of faith took up this challenge the world and its people would not be as divided, suffering and strife-ridden as they are today. And how many people of faith may be included amongst those promoting the evil the god is seeking to destroy?

On Thursday 21 November 2003, at least 27 people were killed, including the Consul General, and hundreds of people were injured in Istanbul when two suicide bombers attacked the British consulate and the HSBC bank. Most of the people who were killed were Turkish Muslims, but the attack was aimed at a British corner of Istanbul, at British culture and government and at those associated with Britain in the area.

The attack was timed to coincide with the visit to Britain of the President of the USA, George W. Bush. An anonymous telephone caller claimed responsibility for the carnage on behalf of al-Qa'ida, the Muslim terrorist group founded by Osama bin Laden, and the Turkish group called the Islamic Great Eastern Raiders' Front. The

American President and the British Prime Minister promised to stand together against the 'fanatics of terror'.

The attacks came only five days after two synagogues had suffered suicide bombings, also in Istanbul. There had also been the destruction of part of a Jewish school in Paris and many smaller attacks on Jewish targets.

Since the 9/11 attack on the World Trade Center in New York and the Pentagon, which were attacks against American culture but also against the whole of the western world by the al-Qa'ida Muslim terrorist network, terrorists have wrought destruction in many places. The western world's response has included the invasion of Iraq and the building up of strategies for hoped-for future protection.

In March 2002 a car bomb detonated near the US embassy in Lima in Peru, killing 9 people and wounding 30 people. In April 2002 a bomb in a lorry detonated close to a synagogue in Djerba in Tunisia. Twenty people were killed.

In May 2002 a car rammed a bus full of French defence technicians in Karachi, killing 14 people. In June 2002 a car was driven into the US consulate, also in Karachi, and the exploding bomb killed 11 people and wounded 45 people.

In October 2002 two bombs exploded in the nightclub area of Bali. A second bomb exploded outside the US consulate. The death toll was 202.

In November 2002 two missiles just missed an Israeli airliner in Mombasa, but a car bomb exploded outside a hotel used by Israeli visitors. Fifteen people were killed.

In May 2003 suicide bombers detonated four bombs in expatriate residential areas in Riyadh. Thirty-five people were killed. Since then Saudi Arabia has suffered many attempted atrocities carried out by Muslim extremists inspired by al-Qa'ida.

Also in May 2003 five bombs exploded near to Jewish and western targets in Casablanca. Forty-five people were killed and 60 wounded.

In June 2003 a car bomber blew up a bus full of German peacekeepers in Kabul. Five people were killed.

In August 2003 a car bomb exploded on the forecourt of the Marriott Hotel in Jakarta. Ten people were killed and 150 wounded.

Also in August 2003 a lorry bomb destroyed the UN headquarters in Baghdad, killing 22 people. Many more people, Iraqi and foreign, have been killed in Iraq since the ending of the war that toppled Sadam Hussain. The murder of Americans in Falluja led to fierce reprisals

In November 2003 there was a suicide bomb onslaught on a residential area in Riyadh. Seventeen people were killed.

On 11 March 2004 a series of bombs exploded on 4 commuter trains going into Madrid and 192 people were killed. Another bomb was found unexploded on the railway line to Madrid.

In August 2004 arsonists attacked a Jewish community in Paris and daubed Nazi symbols on the walls, doors and furniture. The community centre, the site of an old synagogue, is on the first floor of a six-storey building. One of its services is to offer kosher food for old and deprived Jewish people. A week earlier than this attack antisemitic slogans had been written on a wall in front of Notre Dame Cathedral. In 2004 alone more than 300 Jewish graves were desecrated in eastern France.

Five Jewish cemeteries were desecrated in Britain in 2004. On 9 June 2005 100 Jewish graves were desecrated in a cemetery in Prestwich in the heart of Manchester's Orthodox Jewish community. Many gravestones were deliberately smashed, leaving the community shocked and very worried for the future.

On 7 July 2005 four bombs planted by suicide bombers exploded in central London, three on the underground and one on a bus. Fifty-two people were killed and 700 were wounded. The al-Qa'ida network accepted responsibility for the carnage, blamed the British government policies in Afghanistan and the Middle East, and forecast more attacks.

This list of just some recent atrocities is a painful reminder that hatred and violence between people is terrible and prolific, and there is also the on-going violence and destruction in many parts of the world, not least in the Middle East. 'Progress' seems to be less in the development of listening, trust, and shared and loving work, and more in ways of cruelty and of destroying God's people and God's world. One new factor at the beginning of the twenty-first century is that communication and travel are easier than ever before and the tools of destruction are easy to attain and use, whether by suicide bombers or by unscrupulous governments.

There are many causes of all the division, suffering and strife, including poverty, greed, clashes of culture and religion itself. Hatred between people of faith seems particularly cruel, whether today or throughout the history of humankind. Sadly, by 1998 it was estimated that at least half the 30 most dangerous groups in the world were religious.[1]

Many people would argue that faith is not the cause of today's atrocities. Some argue this because they think that religion is not important enough now to be the cause of so much hatred and destruction, and that to focus on it simply hides the real causes, which are political, social and economic. Many religious leaders of all the faiths also tend to argue that the violence is not caused by religion or by its followers. They should perhaps say that violence *should* not be caused by religion or by its followers. Religion at its best should bring holiness, goodness and bravery, and the bravery should surely be in support of the quality of life that all the faiths uphold, of peace with justice for all, of all faiths and of none.

If there is any comfort in the midst of the never-ending catalogue of violence and suffering in the world it is in God who, Christians believe, is always there, in the suffering and in the people who stand out in their opposition to it. These people who cry out for peace and justice exist in all the situations and faiths I touch on, and in so many more. It should never be forgotten that in every situation of division, suffering and strife, there are people of faith who are working for unity, healing and harmony. They are the hope for the future of the world.

The hope must be that the people of faith who work for listening, sharing, trusting and working together with others will be more committed and hard-working than those who are causing divisions and strife by working for the supremacy of their own faiths and cultures over others. The problem is that very often the line between one group, the listeners, and the other, the oppressors, is very blurred and sometimes people may move from one group to another when they or circumstances change. All people, made in the image of God, are capable of love, service and sacrifice. Sadly, the same people are also capable of condoning atrocities and even of direct cruelty. Atrocities go on all the time in the early twenty-first century world and no one can say, 'We do not know.' Sometimes it is easy to condemn violence from a distance of space or time, but to do nothing when it is happening in the present. At the time in 1994 when *Schindler's List*, a novel by Thomas Keneally about one man's efforts to save Jews from death in Nazi Germany, was attracting large audiences in Europe, a shocking genocide was devastating Rwanda, a country which is 95 per cent Christian.

Many people, including myself, would wish to acknowledge that some people of faith are in fact a major cause of many of today's atrocities. They sadly point out that many of the war-torn situations of today are inextricably linked to one of the main world faiths, most of which have a long history of being involved in conflict. They point to Christian members of the IRA, who always thought that their cause of the unity of Ireland was worth killing for. In the Rwandan genocide of 1994 Christians killed Christians. The Muslim terrorists, from Saudi Arabia and around the world, and largely trained in Afghanistan, are keen to take responsibility for much of the recent death and destruction I have listed. Much of the continued fighting and destruction in Iraq since the invasion and ending of the dictatorship is partly caused by instability and insecurity and the resulting poverty, but there is a strong underlying religious current which was held in check in the past by fear of Sadam Hussain. Religious divisions are now causing terrible violence as the Shi'a Muslim majority seeks dominance. This is especially evident in the struggle that has taken place during the shaping and implementation of the constitution.

There are Jews who think that the preservation of Israel is worth killing for. Sinhala Buddhists in Sri Lanka have fought for the survival of their religion and culture against the equally fanatical and destructive Tamil Tigers, who are mostly Hindu. Serbian Christians have targeted and killed Muslims in Bosnia and later in Kosovo. The 1995 massacre of thousands of Muslim men and boys in Srebrenica has been described as the worst single atrocity in Europe since World War Two. Some Sikhs justify killing those who oppose them in their battle for a Sikh homeland of Kalistan in the Punjab. The seeds of the current turmoil in Kashmir were sown when a mainly Muslim population was taken into mainly Hindu India at the time of the partition of India and Pakistan. Hindu nationalists kill Muslims and Christians in India today. The list is long and depressing and could be even longer.

Religious faith is vitally important to its followers and it has been and still is a cause of many of the divisions, sufferings and strife-torn situations in the world. The reason for this seems to be that often the people who become so committed to their particular faith and to the violent causes associated with it have, perhaps without realizing it, obsessively focused on one or two aspects of the faith to the exclusion of other aspects.

Many of today's people of violence say that they are inspired by their faith to do what other people regard as terrible things. There have been many recent interviews with terrorists and most of them bring out the sincerity and commitment they have to their faith. They see themselves as God's agents in transforming the world, which they see as evil. The problem is that they have a very narrow focus on the teachings of their faith and they go on to claim truth and therefore to imply superiority over and suspicion of others. They have no idea at all of listening to others, even those of their own faith who offer them a more rounded but also perhaps a more complicated view of their faith in all its aspects. A 22-year-old Palestinian member of Hamas said when interviewed:

> You don't choose to be a *shaheed* (suicide bomber).
> Allah chooses you. It's a long road to *shahada*. I
> don't know whether my operation will involve a
> settlement or a bus. The leadership takes care of
> that. My family does not know I'm involved. Of
> course, separation will be difficult for them, but in
> the afterlife I will be their saviour. I will take them
> to paradise with me. Knowing that will give them
> solace. The goal of any operation is to kill as many
> people as possible. We don't differentiate – soldiers
> or civilians. The Israelis don't make distinctions
> when they kill Palestinians, so why should we? I'd be
> happy to kill Israeli women and children.[2]

Hala Jaber wrote in *The Sunday Times* about her journey to meet young Palestinian women who are training to be suicide bombers.[3] After many struggles she was allowed to meet nine of the young women secretly and to watch their training. The number of Palestinian women in training is growing, including young mothers. They shared their reasons for wanting to become suicide bombers, including despair for the future and also anger and a wish for revenge for what had happened to their families. One woman had five children but her father, her husband, and two of her brothers had been killed by Israeli forces. The desire for martyrdom and paradise was also strong in the women. The suicide bombers, male and female alike, believe that they will be welcomed to paradise by 70 beautiful nymphs who will wipe away their sins, open the gates of heaven and give them every pleasure, leading to fulfilment and delight.

The young Palestinians, and many other terrorists in the Middle East and elsewhere, seem to ignore the main focus of the teachings of their scriptures and faith leaders, which concentrate on God's love for all people and for all the world, and on the need for love and compassion in people of faith. They have a narrow certainty about what they are doing that is very frightening, perhaps arising out of a need to have a special role in life and even in death. They have not understood that a faith path cannot be based on certainty, for if it is then there is no need for faith.

There may be a warning here for all those of any religion who are dogmatic about faith, using it to oppress others with their tongues if not with bombs and bullets.

Karen Armstrong has published a book on fundamentalism in Christianity, Islam and Judaism.[4] The name 'fundamentalist' came from conservative American theologians who published a series of pamphlets, 'The Fundamentals', between 1910 and 1915. She traces the history of the development of fundamentalism in the three faiths, going back to 1492 CE, and then she goes on to look at its great leap forward in the 1930s and on into the late twentieth century, mostly in reaction to increased secularism. She outlines the growth of fundamentalism, and also opposition to it, in four countries: Israel, Egypt, the USA and Iran towards the end of the twentieth century. She ends with an appeal for toleration, moderation and compassion. But the battle between openness to other faiths and fundamentalism goes on.

Dogmatic religious certainty is perhaps especially attractive to people suffering from unhappiness, loneliness, boring work or no work at all. One of the Palestinian women suicide bombers in training who was interviewed by Hala Jaber said that she had become desperate through the loss of her brother and felt like a prisoner because of the checkpoints. She had completely abandoned any hope of marriage and a family. Some of the people who turn to religious fanaticism and violence do so in the hope of being accepted into a community, however temporary, and of finding a mission and a purpose in life. This seems to be true of many of the young men who have found Osama bin Laden's message attractive and who have gone to Afghanistan to be trained as terrorists.

It is hard for most people of the world faiths to face up to the fact that religion, including their own religion, sometimes has such a negative influence on its adherents, that it causes suffering to those who are different, and that this has always been the case, from the dawn of humanity. I have affirmed the gift of difference between the world faiths in other chapters of this book and the need for people of faith to listen to each other, to develop understanding, trust and to work together. There are many people who are toiling for this. Sadly there are others who are far from being listeners. Those who build walls between the faiths and cultures rather than building bridges suffer from the delusion that their own religion and way of life is somehow not simply unique, but actually superior to other religions and ways of life. They are those who, perhaps because they believe that they have the truth, do not listen to others but, rather, demonize them. Sometimes this delusion extends to different groups within the same religion. The devastation this attitude has caused between Protestants and Roman Catholics within the Christian community in Ireland is obvious.

Saudi Arabia is one country that has built a wall between itself and the rest of the world, particularly in terms of culture and religion, believing that because the Muslim faith began on its soil it has a special role in protecting it from any other influence. No other religion may be practised openly in the country. Anglican Christians gather privately under the title of the Canterbury Community because they are not allowed to use the word 'Christian'. Other Christian groups and members of other faiths also have to meet privately.

It seems strange that on one level Saudi Arabia is ultra-modern and strongly linked to much of the developed world through trade, especially in oil. It is an oil-rich nation with more than 25 per cent of the world's oil reserves. It has a modern and well-equipped military regime and a welfare system. It has more modern luxury perhaps than any other country in the world. It is a country of booming cities dotted around in a sea of desert and mountains, where most people now take mobile phones, big American cars, shopping malls and bright lights, music and sport for granted. The desert nomads, the Bedouin, are in a small minority today, though there are many who live on the edges of the cities. Since 1938 when the first commercial oil well was sunk, leading on to the 1970s oil boom and beyond, the country has become a major ally of the United States and of the UK. It is a country ruled by a wealthy tribal monarchy that came to power early in the twentieth century through military force. The King appoints the Majlis ash-Shura, the consultative assembly created in 1992.

Saudi Arabia is also the birthplace of Osama bin Laden and 15 of the 9/11 hijackers. It is a country facing in two different directions. It is the home of terrorists and it is also the victim of their terror.

It is governed by sharia or Islamic law and has the *mutawaeen* or state religious police to make sure that the law is kept. The headquarters for the *mutawaeen* and the Ministry for Religious Affairs is Riyadh, a centre for Wahhabism, a particularly strict and puritanical form of Islam. Saudi Arabia has Muslim missionaries and has built mosques throughout the Muslim world and beyond. It has the Muslim holy cities, Mecca and Medina, and is therefore the destination for over two million Muslim pilgrims from all over the world every year. The pilgrimage or Haj is one of the Five Pillars of Islam, ordained in the Qur'an. It is one of the main duties of all Muslims who can afford it and are in good health.

The emergence of terrorists in Saudi Arabia is not simply caused by a narrow and comfortable religious upbringing. The country is the temporary home of more than six million guest workers, including both highly skilled professional people who live in luxury and also those from the developing world who do the work most Saudi Arabians do not wish to do, including lorry driving, factory work and other manual labour, domestic service and work in shops.

The Saudi population has grown very quickly since 1970 and is now more than 24 million people with the average woman having 6 children. A generation of Saudi young people has been created who do no work, boys and girls, men and women alike. Fifteen per cent of the overall population is unemployed but 30 per cent of those between 20 and 24 years are unemployed. One of the problems is that many young people have first degrees, but they are often in subjects like Islamic studies. There are not enough people with either practical or professional training in useful fields. Young people are well provided for but most of them are also idle and bored. For some of them this frustration has led them to seek meaning in the philosophy and activities of al-Qa'ida. The Saudi Government is trying to replace some of the foreign workers with Saudi nationals but so far this is not very successful, especially amongst private employers.

It seems clear that one of the aims of al-Qa'ida is to get rid of the Saudi royal family as part of its campaign against the western world. It deliberately sets out to recruit the bored young people who abound in Saudi Arabia and is successful with enough of them to continue its terrorist attacks. It gives them a community, a cause and, through their faith, a zeal that enables them to sacrifice themselves.

The Palestinian suicide bombers are also those who feel that their only hope in a bleak world is their faith and the opportunity they have to give themselves up for it. The government of Israel has responded by attempting to build a huge wall around the Palestinian areas, designed to protect the people of Israel and to separate the Palestinian and Jewish people from each other for ever. The wall is eight metres high and includes electric fences, trenches, cameras, sensors and security patrols. Many Palestinian people have lost their land to the wall, which is not in a straight line but has offshoots and spurs, ruthlessly encircling and dividing the people and scarring the landscape.

The Israeli wall of separation is widely believed to be a big mistake that cannot bring peace to the people of either Israel or Palestine. In a conversation with Prince Hassan of Jordan, on the occasion of the launch in December 2003 of a United Nations declaration of solidarity between people of faith, the Chief Rabbi, Dr Jonathan Sacks, said that his hope was that the wall would come down, but for this to happen people would have to go under and over it, and not let it get in the way of working for understanding and peace. The International Court of Justice in the Hague has condemned the wall and is working through the United Nations to have it demolished.

The Israeli government has built the wall out of desperation, wrong as most of the world community believes it to be. The Jewish people still seem to be among the most vulnerable to attack, and not just in the Middle East. In November 2003 an opinion poll of EU citizens stated that Israel was seen as the greatest danger to world peace. There is fear among Jewish people of a revival of the hatreds of the past. 'Anti-Semitism has become politically correct in Europe', said Natan Sharansky, the former Soviet dissident.[5] The frequent attacks on Jewish people in France which I touched on at the beginning of this chapter are a sad reminder that Sharansky is not exaggerating. Some Jewish people would say that anti-Semitism never went away, but has always been there, even though there have been all the recent efforts of theologians and others to help Christians and Jews to appreciate each other.[6] There has also been the work of organizations like the Council for Christians and Jews.

The Jewish people have faced persecution at the hands of Christians since the beginning of the Church, including the attacks of many of the early fathers and also of Martin Luther at the time of the Reformation. It almost seemed that Jesus the Jew, the link person between Jews and Gentiles, had been forgotten. Medieval England experienced pogroms and the publication of horrible cartoons against the Jews. The Christian condemnation of the Jews was that above all they failed to recognize the Messiah, and many historians feel that this contributed to the evils of the Holocaust.[7]

It is estimated that more than six million Jews died in the Holocaust, murdered in their own countries, in ghettos that had been set up to control them, on the journeys to the camps, and in the camps themselves, places of terror like Dachau and Belsen, Gardelegen and Ohrdruf, Buchenwald and Sachsenhausen, Ravensbruck and Flossenburg, Auschwitz and others.[8]

Hitler's attack against the Jews was intended to wipe them and everything associated with them out; it was to be the 'final solution', and most of those who tried to bring it about were ordinary people who saw themselves as good citizens and who went home to their ordinary families. They would not have thought of themselves as evil, but as simply doing their duty.

Even when World War Two ended, the suffering of the Jewish people did not end, as many of the survivors had nowhere to go and were turned away from many countries when they did try to find a home.[9] Jews escaping from Europe at the end of the war were even turned away from Palestine, the land where they had been promised a home by the British government in the Balfour Declaration of 1919.

The formation of the state of Israel in 1948 and the turmoil that surrounded it has complicated and damaged the relationship between Christians, Jews and Muslims enormously. Jews have longed for Muslims and Christians to relate well to Israel and to understand their love of the land there, following their long and painful exile in so many places and over so many years. Since the formation of Israel many Jews have gone there from all over the world, including more than 12,000 from Russia. The violence that surrounded the birth of the country, when an estimated 750,000 Palestinian people lost their villages and homes, has made it very hard for people to build bridges, though many, of all the faiths in the region, have tried.

Najwa Farah is a good friend, a Palestinian Christian, who has written about becoming a refugee in 1947: 'We were cut off from the world of the living and imprisoned in caves and camps, our condition deteriorating from one crisis to another ... bewildered, shocked, broken-hearted, humiliated ...'[10]

Elias Chacour is another Palestinian Christian, a Melkite priest, who has written about his people being displaced in 1948, about how his father was taken away and their family village destroyed. He is someone who has sought to build bridges of reconciliation between the communities of faith, and this hope continues in his secondary school and new university at Ibillin in Galilee. He always writes of the Muslim and Jewish people as his brothers and sisters and asks all who work for peace and human rights in the region to work for the people of all the faiths who live there.[11]

In the 1967 war the West Bank was taken from Jordan by Israel and soon Israeli settlements sprang up and Palestinian villages were destroyed, as were the beloved olive trees. Israel established a military rule in Gaza, taken from Egypt, and united Jerusalem, a city sacred to Christians, Jews and Muslims, by taking over East Jerusalem.

When Israel was formed Palestinian Christians were 30 per cent of the population of the new Israel, and now they are less than 1 per cent because they have moved to live all over the world. The Palestinian Christian diaspora has been the result of a long struggle for identity by the Christians, who are a minority both in the country and as Palestinians. The increasing violence has also driven many Christian and Muslim people out to live all over the world as well as in the refugee camps of Lebanon and Jordan, the West Bank and Gaza. Today the refugee camps are horrendous places to live in. There can be as many as 13 people sharing a room infested with rats. The schools and clinics are grim places with meagre resources.

Divisions, sufferings and strife have grown since 1967 as Israel has tried to control the entire region by the strategic building of settlements and roads, what has come to be known as the 'matrix of control'. This means that although the Palestinians have land and homes in what is now Palestine they are not free to move about from one area to another and have no real control. Gaza has been regularly sealed off, as are the other Palestinian areas, and work, family life and the Palestinian economy have all suffered. Currently the water is piped away from the West Bank and then sold back to the Palestinians. There is a huge problem of poverty among the Palestinians, with at least 20 per cent of them living below the poverty line.[12]

Since September 2000 the second intifada has risen up and the violence in the region and the suicide bombings have escalated, usually followed by harsh reprisals by the Israeli government.

It is not only the Palestinian people who condemn the Israeli government's harsh regime. Avraham Burg, Speaker of the Knesset from 1999 to 2003, wrote in *The Guardian* in September 2003, 'The Jewish people did not survive for two millennia in order to pioneer new weaponry, computer security programmes or anti-missile missiles. We were supposed to be a light unto the nations. We have failed.' In the same article he wrote of the suicide bombers:

Israel, having ceased to care about the children of the Palestinians, should not be surprised when they come washed in hatred and blow themselves up in the centres of Israeli escapism. They consign themselves to Allah in our places of recreation, because their own lives are torture. They spill their own blood in our restaurants in order to ruin our appetites, because they have parents and children at home who are hungry and humiliated.[13]

Avraham Burg is one of many Jewish people who have sympathy for the situation of the Palestinian people, and I write about some of them in Chapter 6. There are members of Peace Now, connected with the Labour Party, and members of many other radical Jewish groups, including Gush Shalom, the Arab and Jewish Israeli group, Taayush, and B'Tselem which collects and publishes data. Physicians for Human Rights does excellent work in the medical field. The Committee Against House Demolitions initiates the rebuilding of homes that have been destroyed by the army. Rabbis for Human Rights represents the religious community that does not follow the fanatical nationalist banner. Machsom Watch tries to stop abuses at the checkpoints; Yesh Gvul helps the increasing number of soldiers who refuse to serve in the occupied areas.

The Jewish people working for peace are a wonderful sign of hope in a region of despair and suffering. Some of them go out to help village people who are stopped from picking their olives in October every year. They form a human shield and pick the olives. This is a strong public demonstration of solidarity with the Palestinian people for whom the olive tree is an ancient source of livelihood and a vital peace symbol. The loss of hundreds of olive trees and separation from many of the remaining trees has caused great unhappiness. A group of writers also organizes olive-picking sessions, including Amos Oz, David Grossman, A. B. Yehoshua and Me'ir Shalev.

The Israeli government has attracted some sympathy and hope for peace around the world with the withdrawal of its settlers from Gaza, though this seems, sadly, to be part of the overall plan to completely separate the Israeli people from the Palestinian people and to strengthen the Israeli presence elsewhere, including the West Bank. Until 15 August 2005 there were 21 Jewish settlements in Gaza, with about 8,000 settlers, making up 2 to 3 per cent of the total Israeli settler population. The 21 settlements have been closed down, together with 4 settlements in the West Bank. The settlers were asked to leave with compensation, and most did so, sadly but peacefully, while others, both secular and religious, refused to leave and demonstrated their anger and sense of betrayal. They were supported by people from other areas of Israel, especially young people who were strengthened by knowing that the closures coincided with Tisha B'av, when Jews remember the destruction of the temple in Jerusalem. It is said that about 50,000 Israeli police and soldiers were involved in the operation, including the removal of the people who refused to leave and the demolition of their beautiful houses.

There is the great fear that anti-Semitism is growing in Europe and there is also another great fear, that the western world is building a wall of prejudice against Muslims and the Muslim world. The western media is rarely positive about Muslim people and issues; they are mostly depicted as alien, fanatical and wrong. One exception to this was the publicity given to the two members of the Muslim Council of Great Britain who travelled to Iraq in October 2004 to try to save Kenneth Bigley, the captured British hostage. The fact that they failed did not detract from their brave efforts. Another exception has been the publicity given to some British Muslims following the London bombings of 7 July 2005, when many of them came forward to denounce the terror. There is normally little attention in the press to the majority of peaceful British Muslims who are now being encouraged to protest when they are stereotyped as bigoted and militant. It is true, as we have already seen, that there are extreme and fanatical Muslims, like the Palestinian suicide bombers and members and supporters of the al-Qa'ida network, and that they have a high profile in the world's media. It is also true that there are many conflicts in the Islamic world, including Palestine, Iraq, Afghanistan, Chechnya, Pakistan and Kashmir. However, we have seen that Islam is not the only faith to have been badly used by governments and their opponents and badly represented by some of its followers. The majority of Muslims remain moderate, accepting of others and good citizens themselves. One of the problems is that much of the reporting on Muslim areas of the world focuses on religion, while articles on other areas and peoples where there is trouble are more likely to focus on the conflicts, without reference to religion.

The report of the Runnymede Trust, *Islamophobia, a Challenge for Us All*, was published in 1997.[14] The report is very clear that Islamophobia does not include disagreement with Muslim beliefs or practices, nor does it include criticism of Muslim states where internationally recognized human rights are not allowed. Islamophobia includes unfounded and ignorant prejudice and open hostility, and the stereotyping of all Muslims as the same. Islamophobia does not recognize the richness of culture and the diversity to be found in Muslim communities and in the Muslim world or the value of learning from Muslims.

In June 2004 a new report by the Commission on British Muslims and Islamophobia was published, *Islamophobia: Issues, Challenges and Action*.[15] Important developments and progress since 1997 are listed. However, notwithstanding many improvements, including government encouragement to interfaith organizations and meetings, the report also makes it clear that Islamophobia has not been reduced and that in some ways it is worse because Muslims are more in the spotlight than they were before September 11th 2001.

British Muslims have suffered from being pigeonholed in the same box for many years, but recently this has included all the communities being under suspicion of supporting terrorism and of harbouring terrorists.

There are clearly some terrorists who have grown up in Muslim communities in Britain, including those who fought for the Taliban and were sent to Guantanamo Bay; Richard Reid, the shoe bomber; and those involved in the London bombings on 7 July 2005. The police carried out a hunt in some Muslim homes and communities in London, Luton and Lancashire in early August 2004, leading to eight men being charged with conspiracy to murder. One of the people arrested had written a guide to *jihad* which includes practical advice on warfare, including ambushes, raids and moving at speed through mountains. Arrests were made following the 7/7 bombings and following the failed bombing attempts a week later on 14 July.

There seems to be a new trend for a growing number of young British Muslims to turn to extremism, perhaps following their disillusionment when they marched with many other British people against the 2003 invasion of Iraq and were ignored. In 2004 young British Muslims were discovered supporting the Shi'a people of Iraq by their presence in the holy city of Najaf, which became a fortress for Shi'a Islam when the Shi'a Muslim leader Moqtada al-Sadr led what he considered a holy war against the British and American armies and the Iraqi government.

In August 2004 Rory McCarthy wrote in *The Guardian* about two young men, born in Iraq and brought up in London, who had gone to Najaf to join the 'holy war'. He found them being trained in the use of guns. They told him that they received no money and ate only very simple food. They did not approve of terrorism, including the actions of al-Qa'ida, and believed that they were defending the country they were born in. One of the two said, 'We all have a belief ... we asked our families and they said yes. It is good to protect your country and be there with your brothers.'[16]

The British Muslim community has condemned terrorism, through the communities and through the Council of Mosques, and has patiently responded to suspicions in many ways. The Muslim Council of Great Britain, which represents more than 350 Islamic organizations, published a book, *The Quest for Sanity: Reflections on 11 September and the Aftermath*, referred to in Chapter 5. The council has also produced a model sermon in 2004 for imams to use, which makes a clear distinction between the *jihad* or holy war and terrorism.

Jihad is understood as an honourable struggle to defend one's homeland from external attacks. The young men who went to Najaf would see themselves as fitting into this category. Terrorism on the other hand is an attack on innocent people.

The Muslim freedom fighters in the Philippines, on the island of Mindanao, see themselves as waging a holy war, a *jihad*, to win freedom for their people. The members of the Moro Islamic Liberation Front (MILF), formed in 1976, resorted to fighting because they saw no other alternative. They, the Muslims of Mindanao, were there long before the Spanish conquest of 1521, which gave the Philippines its name and which introduced the Roman Catholicism that is now embraced by about 85 per cent of the people.

A symbol of new life may be seen in the mosque that has been built within Fort Pikit, a fort built in the Spanish era and therefore representing colonialism and oppression. The fort is on a hill overlooking the town and is now a new sign of hope for the Muslim people.

The Muslims are 7 per cent of the population. They feel that the independence of the Philippines in 1946, which included Mindanao, was as negative an event as the Spanish conquest because the Muslim people of Mindanao were never considered as a separate group with special gifts and needs. At the same time they are in reality a separate group, culturally and geographically. When I visited the Philippines in the autumn of 2003 as the guest of the United Church of Christ in the Philippines, most of the programme was in Mindanao but I never met a Muslim person. The church members were also interested in meeting Muslims and in understanding and working with them, but said that in the current situation it was extremely difficult.

The MILF does try to negotiate and work with the government and some Muslim peace zones have been established. There is also the Abubakre Camp in the south-west of Mindanao, which is a peaceful and vision-filled Muslim town, including a mosque, homes, farms and an Islamic university. The efforts of MILF are often halted by the terrorism of the more extremist groups, especially the Abu Sayaff Group, which detonates bombs and kidnaps people from time to time, including foreign tourists. They are the Muslims of the Philippines who are likely to be reported in the world press.

Muslims everywhere now fear the way the media may represent them. The Muslim Council of Great Britain shares this fear and is constantly working to help British Muslims to overcome it. In the autumn of 2004 every Muslim household in Britain received a booklet called *Know Your Rights and Responsibilities*, prepared by the council. The booklet urges Muslims to take part fully in British national life, including joining one of the main political parties. They are asked to inform the police if they have any suspicion of any terror-related activity. Interviews with Muslims following the 7/7 London bombings made clear the fact that some Muslims would find this difficult. One man said that if he suspected anyone of being a terrorist he would get the community to stop the terrorism but that he would not tell the police.

Mosque committees are asked to consider installing CCTV and to be on the lookout for suspicious packages. The booklet also warns Muslims of the danger of revenge attacks following the violence of the Muslim terrorists around the world. Women who wear obvious Muslim dress including the hijab are warned to think twice about going out alone. This warning was reiterated after the 7/7 London bombings when there were, sadly, some revenge attacks on Muslim communities and individuals. Dr Zaki Badawi, the late prominent Muslim, said in a television interview that Islam gives Muslim women the choice between wearing Muslim headdress and not wearing it.

Polly Toynbee, writing in *The Guardian* in August 2004, saw things from a different perspective when she challenged moderate Muslims to protest much more loudly against terror around the world. She also raised her fear that it is increasingly difficult to champion liberalism and human rights, including the equality of the sexes, without being seen as working against traditional Muslims.[17]

Most of the Muslims in Britain originated in Pakistan or Bangladesh. The Pakistani community in Britain may be found in most major cities, including Bradford, Birmingham, Manchester, London, Rochdale, Oldham, Glasgow, Edinburgh and Leicester. Most of the community came to Britain in the early 1950s, to work in jobs that were vacant, mainly in factories. Most of them came from large extended families in rural areas. They found it hard to integrate into the surrounding British community at first, because many of them did not speak English. They also brought their strong cultural traditions with them. When they married they did so in the traditional way, through their families, in Britain or in their original homelands.

Monica Ali's novel *Brick Lane* is a story about a traditional Muslim marriage, arranged between Bangladesh and London.[18] The central character in the story is Nazneen, who is 18 years old when she is married to a much older man. She comes from a village in Bangladesh to live in east London and the novel is about her struggle to make sense of her traditional life in a western capital city. With the help of her British-born daughters, she at last manages to become a real person and to feel in control of her life.

The second generation of British Muslims has been educated and some of them are members of the professions and thus of the British middle class. The conflicts within the community are mostly about issues of land in Pakistan. Religion is most important in the community, and also a source of disagreement because some people belong to one of the Sufi orders while others oppose Sufism. The most prominent anti-Sufi group is the Wahhabi group, which spread from Arabia to India in the nineteenth century. It is strict and puritanical and one of the most influential groups in Saudi Arabia.

Dudley in the West Midlands has what is in most ways a typical Muslim community, which originated in the Mirpur area of Pakistan's neighbour, Kashmir. At the end of November 2003 two young Muslim men were arrested in Dudley as part of a nationwide anti-terrorist sweep. A third man from Dudley was arrested in Walsall with a man from Luton. Before there was even time for the men to be charged, a few members of the Dudley white community reacted by shooting into a row of Asian businesses and by destroying cars in the street that included the homes of two of the men who had been arrested.

The attacks on the Muslim community in Dudley were attacks on people who have worked especially hard to be part of the wider community they live in and who, since September 11th 2001, have spoken out against terrorism and organized memorials for all those who were killed. The young men who were arrested attended a very orthodox mosque which follows the puritanical tradition that developed in nineteenth-century India. The imam came from Saudi Arabia. He is very clear that terrorism is outlawed by Islam. The community has been devastated and is in grave danger of being torn apart, as are many other Muslim communities in the UK.

As in Saudi Arabia so in Britain, religion is not the only reason for fanaticism amongst young people. The young Muslims living in Dudley have the highest levels of unemployment in the region. The same is true in Muslim communities right across the country. Further, young Muslim graduates everywhere in Britain find it much harder to find employment than white students.

The Muslim community in Dudley has not given up hope. There are plans for a beautiful new mosque which will be a gift to the town. The mosque will include a community and enterprise centre for Muslims and non-Muslims. A tribute has been made to Christianity through the windows of the mosque which resemble cathedral windows. The mosque will celebrate Christmas as well as the Muslim festivals.

It is a depressing fact that Christians in Pakistan do not feel such friendliness from most of the Muslims who make up the majority of the population there.

Pakistan means 'land of the pure'. It was founded in 1947 and 97 per cent of the people are Muslim, the vast majority being Sunni Muslim.[19] 'Pakistan is more than a country it is also an idea, a cultural expression of identity.'[20] The All India Muslim League was founded in 1906. In the 1930s Mohammed Ali Jinnah became the Muslim leader and began to work for a separate Muslim state. The partition of India and Pakistan took place in 1947 when more than 2 million people were killed and 15 million people moved from their homes. Hindus went to India and Muslims to Pakistan. The partition was a catastrophic failure for many people who had worked for the integration of the communities, not least Mahatma Gandhi. Jinnah did try to give freedom and peace to minorities but his work did not outlive him. He died in September 1948 and since then Pakistan has been troubled, its people suffering more as the years have gone on. When elections were finally held in 1970, following a long period of martial law, East Pakistan voted in the Awami League under Sheikh Mujibur Rahman. He was arrested and a government in exile was established in Calcutta. About 11 million refugees moved from East Pakistan to West Bengal, which prompted the Indian government to invade East Pakistan. By December 1971 Pakistan had surrendered and Bangladesh had been born. There is the feeling among historians that when Pakistan lost this war there was a loss of confidence among Muslims and that this is one reason why they became more intolerant in their developing and increasingly Islamic country.

Christians in Pakistan have mostly been converted to their faith over the last 200 years from the poorer groups in the country. They have always been isolated and often persecuted by a minority of fanatical Muslims. Most ordinary Muslims have been saddened by the suffering of the Christians. Some Muslims have also suffered from persecution. A Muslim academic visited the USA in the aftermath of September 11th 2001 to be with the American people and to speak in churches. He shared his Muslim faith and explained that his understanding of *jihad* or struggle is that it is a struggle by each person with him or herself, the struggle to be a better Muslim, working for peace and justice.

The amendments to the 1973 constitution and the enforcement of the sharia laws has perhaps contributed most to the marginalization of Christians in Pakistan. One example of change is that in 1979 the word 'freely' in relation to the practice of faith was removed from the constitution. Another change is that Christians are not allowed to represent Muslims in Parliament but vote on a national basis for Christian representatives in the National Assembly, so that local MPs do not necessarily see the need to help Christians in their areas.

The Blasphemy Law has been a hard one for Christians to live under and since 1991 it includes the direction that the punishment for insults to Islam or to the Prophet of Islam should be capital punishment. A report on the work of the Blasphemy Law has recommended that the death sentence should be abolished for those convicted.[21] The Roman Catholic Bishop of Faislabad, John Joseph, shot himself when Ayub Masih was sentenced to death under the Blasphemy Law in 1998.

Most of the Muslims in Pakistan are sad and also ashamed about the attacks on Christians in their country. The President of Pakistan, Pervez Musharraf, has condemned the killings and general hostility to Christians. The suffering and persecution of minorities in Pakistan have, however, increased since September 11th 2001, because many Muslims have been outraged by the Pakistan government's support for America in fighting terrorism. The events of September 11th 2001 led to a complete and dramatic change of direction for a government that had previously supported the Taliban in Afghanistan and had admired Osama bin Laden. America's uncompromising ultimatum to Pakistan and its attack on Afghanistan made it easy for the President to decide where he thought the interests of his country were best served. Pakistan has since then caught more than 500 suspected and wanted terrorists and has worked consistently with the West in seeking to destroy al-Qa'ida. Information has been passed readily to the USA and to the UK, so that President Musharraf has been given the name 'Busharraf' by some groups.

However, many people point out that General Musharraf has not tackled some of his own internal extremist groups in the way that he has tackled the international groups. The problem is that there may be links and common ground between all Muslim terrorists, although since 7 July 2005 this is thought less likely. There is so far no evidence that the London bombers had a direct link with Pakistan and its *madrassahs*. The breeding ground of religious extremism is said to be in the *madrassahs*, the Muslim schools, which are said to number 12,000, and which flourish and are encouraged in Pakistan, not always focusing on the peaceful aspects of faith.

Lord Ahmed, a Muslim member of the House of Lords who works for race relations and human rights, has said that British Muslim society is also in danger because many imams are preaching messages of division, exclusion and hatred in mosques and *madrassahs*. He has suggested that imams should be able to speak English and should have some knowledge of British culture before they are appointed. Research carried out by the BBC following 7 July 2005 made it clear that many Muslims agree with Lord Ahmed and would, further, want to insist that imams should preach in English.

Mahatma Gandhi believed that every person of faith should work to be a better person of his or her own faith and to understand other people of other faiths. Gandhi was a Hindu who worked throughout his life to develop understanding and trust between people of all the faiths of India. He was devastated by the partition, which was a terrible failure for his vision and work. He would have been more devastated by the India of the late twentieth and early twenty-first centuries, an India which seems to be divided on faith lines, with persecution and suffering on all sides, but particularly with persecution by some Hindus of some of the Muslim and Christian minorities.

Gandhi might have turned to the early years of Christianity, when Christians went to South India and when some local Hindus decided to join them, as a good example of people of faith living in peace and harmony together. The fact of Christianity as a very early religion in India is well known by the people of South India. The presence of the Syrian Orthodox community today is often referred to as an example of a community that lives with the vast majority of Hindu people around it without attempting to convert them.

The later incursions of Christians and also of Muslims were often less peaceful and less accepting. The Hindu violence against Muslims and Christians in India came to the attention of the wider world in the 1990s, but antagonisms between the faith communities had been there since the arrival of Muslims in the eleventh century and then of Christian groups, from the time of Vasco da

Gama at the end of the fifteenth century and the establishment of the Roman Catholic Church, through the advent of Protestant missionaries and on to the present time.

The feeling of many Hindus has always been that they have been the target of the evangelism of some Christians and Muslims. This has not always been the case. In Chapter 3 I introduced some of the more gracious missioners who went to India, from Catholic and Protestant traditions, to listen and learn and to become part of the communities they lived in.

There is also the feeling among some Hindus that Christians and Muslims are not truly Indian and that their loyalty lies outside the country. It is felt that Muslims are loyal to Muslims around the world, and especially loyal to those in Pakistan. Christians are loyal to worldwide Christianity; Roman Catholics are also loyal to the Vatican. There is not the same antagonism to Buddhism, which developed from within India and from a Hindu root. The tribal and Dalit people who become Buddhist are accepted by the Hindu majority much more readily than those who become Muslim and Christian.

Dr Ambedkar is remembered by the Dalits, the poorest and most oppressed people of India, as someone who brought them the hope of freedom and dignity in the years leading up to Indian independence. He was a writer, teacher, political philosopher and humanist. His legal and constitutional expertise led to his overseeing the drafting of the Indian constitution after partition. In his pilgrimage to bring dignity and status to the poor people of India in the 1930s and 1940s, he chose to move from Hinduism to become a Buddhist because he felt that Buddhism was class and caste free, unlike either Christianity or Hinduism.

It is in the areas where there has either been a tradition of rivalry between people of faith or where recent insensitive evangelists have worked that the violence has been greatest.

In 1992 the mosque at Ayodhya was destroyed by Hindus who claimed the site as the birthplace of Lord Rama and said that the earlier Hindu temple had been destroyed by Muslims many centuries ago. The destruction of the mosque sparked violent clashes between the Hindu and Muslim communities which have continued in many areas of India and most recently in Gujarat where hundreds of Muslims were slaughtered for no other reason than their religion. Some Hindus have made plans to rebuild the temple to Lord Rama over the site of the destroyed mosque, though this has so far been forbidden by the Indian government.

Recent attacks against Christians have been largely in areas where missionaries have been openly attempting to convert Hindus and those who are outside caste, now known as the Dalit people, and where tribal people have been converted. Sixty per cent of Christians in India are those who were outside caste, once known as 'untouchable' and now known as the Dalit people, those who are oppressed and crushed. There are regular attacks on Dalits all over India, whether they have been converted to Christianity or not. Many Christians have identified with and championed the Dalit people, the most oppressed, which is one reason why some of the militant Hindus attack them, verbally or physically.

Fifteen per cent of Christians in India are from the tribal or Adivasi group. Some tribal groups are now almost all Christian and are viewed with suspicion by the national government. One reason for this may be that the tribal people are most likely to become Christian as communities rather than as individuals, and are therefore seen as a threat to whole regions where, though they have never been Hindu, they have previously been influenced by Hindu culture.

There have been burnings of churches and violent attacks on Christians in tribal areas, especially in Gujarat. At the end of January 1999 an Australian evangelical missionary who had worked with leprosy patients for about 20 years was murdered with his 2 sons in Orissa in eastern India. They had been to an evangelical rally with tribal people and were asleep in their Land-Rover in the forest when they were burnt to death. There have been many attacks since this one, and the evidence is that they have been well organized and that there has been little effort by the authorities to find the culprits.

Many people inside and outside India would say that people who commit acts of violence or allow the violence to happen cannot be Hindu at all because Hinduism is a peaceful religion, accepting of others. They are those who condemn the attacks on Christians and Muslims and speak up for peaceful co-existence, and they include some religiously conservative Hindu leaders. Many members of this group constitute the left-wing liberal group in India, most well known in the Congress Party. Sanjay Trehan is a Hindu who wrote a poem about his rejection and abhorrence of the violence:

> I renounce religion
> ... that makes bonfires of little children
> torches pregnant women
> turns neighbour against neighbour
> and makes monsters out of ordinary faceless men
> leading dull pitiless lives ...
>
> you scum
> you make me ashamed of being
> I renounce the sordid religion you embody
> religion the slayer of innocent kids
> religion the one way ticket to lunacy
> I renounce you.[22]

This poem could very easily be applied to the behaviour of some other religious people in some other places in the world.

A straightforward and Hindu nationalistic approach is that for Hindus Hinduism is all-embracing, including every aspect of life and of the beyond. From this standpoint members of this group attack the secular constitution of India, seeing it as a vehicle for destroying ancient Hindu values and for undermining old and introducing new foreign values, from other religions and from the secular culture of the western world. They remember the violence and colonization of the past and point to the cultural and economic globalization of the present as threats to their identity. This group wishes to establish a Hindu state and its political expression is through the Bharatiya Janata Party (BJP). The ascendancy of this party is recent but there is a long history of Hindu nationalism.

The 'Back to the Vedas' movement was a nineteenth-century movement led by Swami Dayanand Sarasvati, who founded the Arya Samaj which is still popular. In 1925 the Rashtriya Svayamsevak Sangh (RSS), was formed as a nationalist cultural renewal movement. Many of the pro-Hindutva leaders grew from within this movement. The Vishva Hindu Parishad was founded in 1964 from the RSS and now has branches in many countries, including Britain. Bajrang Dal is a militant youth wing.

In May 2004 the people of India voted for change when the Hindu nationalist BJP alliance was defeated and the Congress Party was voted in to form an alliance of those who support work towards religious tolerance and improvements in the lives of the poor. The new Congress-led alliance campaigned in support of the secular constitution of India, which was framed so that all citizens would have full rights, not determined by faith or by birth into a caste. The election result was a surprise for people in India and throughout the world. The Congress Party campaign was successful because many people, including the Congress Party leader Sonia Gandhi, were outraged by the religious persecution leading to many deaths in the very recent past. They were also offended because the BJP alliance had campaigned on the basis of the improvements it had brought to the lives of the Indian middle classes, without consideration for the poor and downtrodden. Dr Joseph D'Souza, the president of the All India Christian Council, while realizing that the future for India and its people would not be easy, wrote when the election results were announced:

> Civil society is now looking forward to the rejection of the Hindutva agenda that has affected many areas of Indian life. A national anti-conversion law is now out of the question. Most certainly there will be a review of the anti-terrorism laws that have been used to victimize the innocent. Civil society wants immediate review of the education department. Most importantly, the oppressed people, the Dalits, will receive more attention.[23]

India is a land of many contrasts, of noise and of peace, of filth and of beauty, of darkness and of light, of wealth and of poverty, of violence and death, of peace and harmony, of hatred and of love, of good and of evil.

Shiva, the destroyer of evil, is the Lord of the Dance, and his dance is the dance of the cosmos. It is said that when he whirls his trident the lightning flashes, and that he has a third eye burning in the middle of his forehead which may shrivel anything he looks at. It is said that when the oceans were being churned and the mountains were being twisted the serpent Vasuki was suffering such agony that he opened his jaws and torrents of blue venom poured out. The world would have been destroyed if Shiva had not swallowed the poison and saved the world from evil. The poison burned his throat, which turned blue, so that he is always known as the blue-throated one.[24]

The Indian who became world famous through his work for peace and harmony, for new life for the poorest of the poor, for beauty, light and love, was Mahatma Gandhi, a Hindu who was violently killed by another Hindu. Gandhi lived a life and raised a hope for all the people of India which was more down to earth than Shiva's dance in a circle of fire but which was equally powerful in opposing destruction, suffering and strife.

The spinning wheel, now on the flag of India, is symbolic of what Gandhi hoped for, not merely for the people of India but for the people of the world. The simple spinning wheel conveys hope for every person, hope and the real possibility of peace, independence and a livelihood, and thus the hope of dignity, self-respect and respect for others, though today this may come in ways never imagined by Gandhi, through the world of the computer and the internet.

A sign of hope which Gandhi would have recognized and been grateful for is what has happened in the village of Gah in Pakistan. Gah is the village 50 miles south-west of Islamabad where the Sikh Indian Prime Minister who was chosen following the May 2004 elections was born more than 70 years ago. Mammohan Singh was the son of a shopkeeper and attended the village school where he was, according to those who remember him, always top of the class. In 1941 Mammohan Singh's family moved to live in Rawalpindi and he eventually studied at Cambridge University in the UK and went on to be a distinguished economist. He later entered politics and became India's finance minister in the 1990s.

When the Singh family lived in Gah it included Muslims, Sikhs and Hindus, but following the 1947 partition it is totally Muslim. The relationship between India and Pakistan has had more downs than ups in the years since partition, but efforts have recently been made to develop dialogue between the two neighbours about Kashmir and other sensitive issues. Gah is being turned into a model village in honour of Mammohan Singh. The Pakistani government will pay for gas to be installed and also for a sewerage system and telephone lines. Gah is a symbol of new hope.

Alongside the spinning wheel, a symbol of hope for peace and justice between people, communities and countries around the world, is a series of interlocking wheels, where the small wheel turns a larger wheel, and the larger wheel drives an even larger one.

Suffering, destruction and strife are often the direct result of human frailty, very often encouraged by a misguided religious zeal. Challenge and change for the better may come from individuals and faith communities seeking to live in the real world and to change that world by being part of it and thus moving it on, beginning as individuals and small communities and thus also moving much bigger places and issues. The spinning wheel, the interlocking wheels and the ring of fire are linked, and all are needed.

5

Only one world

> Recall the face of the poorest and weakest man whom you may have seen and ask yourself if the step you contemplate is going to be of any use to him.[1]

This challenge by Mahatma Gandhi is a challenge to all people working with those of a faith other than their own. Interfaith work cannot stop with people meeting and sharing information and ideas, but must go on to the same people working together for better communities, countries and their one shared world, in whatever way is necessary.

> No human life together
> without a world ethic for the nations.
> No peace among the nations
> without peace among the religions.
> No peace among the religions
> without dialogue between the religions.
> No dialogue between the religions
> without global ethical standards.
> No survival of our globe
> without a global ethic.[2]

These are some of the words Hans Küng used to end his book *Global Responsibility*.

When the Dalai Lama gave his speech in acceptance of the Nobel Peace Prize he focused on what people of faith have in common, as people, and went on to challenge all people to recognize and respond to their responsibilities for the world. He said, 'We need to cultivate a universal responsibility for one another and the planet we share.'[3] He went on to say that his belief is that religion and spirituality have a greater role to play in the world than ever before and that people of faith must strive to build a better world together, by recognizing that we have the same hopes, dreams and goals, and by strengthening and supporting each other.

The hope of many of those engaged in interfaith work over more than a century has been, like the hope of the Dalai Lama, that people of the world faiths will join together in a common struggle for a better world. A lot of headway has been made, including the development of the worldwide interfaith movement and the establishment of the many interfaith organizations, including the World Congress of Faiths, the World Conference for Religion and Peace and the International Association for Religious Freedom. The Inter Faith Network is a newer organization in the UK. There is also the North American Interfaith Network.

It is important to remember what has been focused on in Chapter 3, that the vast majority of the members of the main world faiths always hope and work for their members to be better members of their own faith. There is no question in the minds of most people of faith of the watering down of faiths into one big stew. The hope is quite the contrary, that the faiths will, through the commitment and convictions of their members, be strong and bold both in the uniqueness of their beliefs and cultures and in their love and care for the world. Part of this hope for most people is now that the people of the faiths may, as members of strong faiths, work together where at all possible.

And people from the unique faiths do also have much in common, which with goodwill may be the basis of shared work. Most people of faith, with the exception of most Buddhists and Jains, recognize God in all things and people and also recognize God as the creator of all that is, which is therefore of supreme importance. Ronald Wynne, a Christian missionary in Botswana, said, 'You never go to a place where God is absent.' The shared beliefs of people of faith inevitably make a difference to their actions for a better world.

Most people of faith today long to be recognized as those for whom religion is vitally important; they long to be seen as partners with members of the majority faith in a country and also with others who are working for a better world, countries and communities.

An English university chaplain told the story of trying to arrange for a meeting between the Christian chaplaincy students and Hindus in the university. He put up a notice in the students' union, announcing the meeting between Christians and Hindus. When he went along at the time arranged he found people spilling out into the corridor outside the room, all Hindu students, while his own Christian students were hidden away in the crowd. He later asked the Hindu students why so many of them had come along and was told that they were so happy to be described through their faith as 'Hindu students' that they came along to the meeting. The usual practice in the university was to describe them as 'Asian students'. They expressed their longing to work together with people of other faiths in the university and in the wider community and country.

There can be nothing outside the concern and responsibility, and prayer, meditation and action, of people of faith. Many people of faith have come to recognize the value of working with those who follow a religious path, for even if it is a different one from their own it will hopefully have a spiritual and unselfish focus.[4]

Shared work between people of the world faiths may be in many areas including community and development projects, ecological issues and reconciliation and peacemaking, locally, nationally and internationally.

The 'Declaration Towards a Global Ethic' was launched by the 1993 gathering of the world religions in Chicago. This statement was the first to be supported by religious leaders from all over the world. It sought to be different from the UN Declaration on Human Rights and to point to much more than rights. The declaration also had to avoid being a political manifesto or a sermon. It further had to avoid matters of disagreement between the faiths, such as divorce. There is no reference to God in the declaration, because this would have made it impossible for most Buddhists to affirm it. Much of the work of putting the declaration into practice has still to be done, and this may be so for a long time. It is nevertheless an important step towards understanding between people of faith. It makes some of the common values and hopes clear, including its affirmation of 'a set of core values in the teachings of the religions'.

The core values shared by the religions of the world include non-violence, equality between people, and the centrality of forgiveness. The declaration is a contribution and encouragement to work for peace and justice at every level in the twenty-first-century world. The full statement is included as Appendix 2 at the end of this book.

Community and development projects have been run by the world faiths for as long as the faiths have existed. Shared projects are newer and have grown up gradually, some having arisen naturally in response to a shared need. In India there are many practical development groups whose members are from all the faiths of India. The Indian interfaith group I know best is the Young Men's Welfare Society in Calcutta, whose members are Christian, Hindu and Muslim. They work together to provide primary health care, education and clean water for many of the poorest people in Calcutta and in the nearby villages.

Much of the community and development work that is shared between the faith groups around the world has grown up since the 1993 declaration. This work has grown in the developing world more quickly than in Britain, because the needs of the developing world are so great and so obvious. Many projects have been initiated by members of one of the faiths, and others have then joined in.

Chaplaincy work in prisons and hospitals in the UK is increasingly organized on an interfaith basis. There is also some shared chaplaincy work between the faiths in some of the universities and colleges. When I visited the Anglican prison chaplains in Brixton prison to learn about their work I was also introduced to the Hindu chaplain, who is the chaplain for all Hindu prisoners in England, so that he moves around every week. He also works with the families of the prisoners.

The law in the UK recognizes a prisoner's right to practise his or her own religion. There are approximately 58,000 people in prison now in England and Wales and two thirds of them register as Christian. There are approximately 4,000 Muslims in prison, 400 Sikhs, 350 Jews, 300 Buddhists and a few Hindus.

The senior and full-time chaplains in the prisons are still likely to be Christian, but since their responsibility is to all the prisoners in the prison they serve in, and also to all staff who work there, they are more and more finding themselves organizing teams of chaplains, including those of the world faiths, some of whom are full-time, some part-time and some voluntary. I have led workshops for prison chaplains of the major world faiths. Their working conditions are very varied. They have in common their commitment to the prisoners and to those working in the prisons. There is much that they may unite to change in the prison system.

The report by the Commission on British Muslims and Islamophobia includes a list of issues that need attention in the prison service. The report is written in relation to Muslims but the issues apply equally to most faiths other than the Christian faith, which is well catered for. The issues include: the timing of prayers, the appointment of suitable 'chaplains' and their training, suitable food, sacred space and festivals. The section on suitable training suggests:

> Appropriate certified training, using a mix of distance learning and residential events, needs to be developed. In addition a multi-faith and inclusive handbook for chaplains, imams and visiting ministers has been issued and a programme of joint national and regional conferences is to be developed.[5]

Teams of hospital chaplains also work on an interfaith basis in the UK, so that patients and their families are cared for by someone of their own faith. The chaplains normally have regular meetings together and there are growing examples of chaplaincy teams producing booklets on the best care and food for their patients, according to their faith. The Brent hospitals are among those that have produced very good booklets, which include recipes and good advice.[6]

Work with asylum seekers in the UK is increasingly done on an interfaith basis. The asylum seekers themselves come from many faiths around the world and it is much more sensible for people of faith to work together on their welcome and care than for this to be done separately.[7] People of faith can also help each other with practical information about what refugees of the faiths can and cannot do within the rules of their faiths, so that the deep unhappiness often caused to many people can be avoided.

One Zimbabwean woman told her story of coming to England from a dire situation where her brother had been killed, the whole family had been threatened and she herself had been followed and threatened until she had left her country in sheer desperation. When she arrived in England she had faced a time of great loneliness, until she joined an interfaith women's support group where she gained new confidence and has succeeded, within two years, in gaining admission to a college where she will be trained as a Methodist minister.

L'Arche is an international federation of communities in which people with mental disabilities and assistants of all faiths live, work and share their lives together. It was founded by Jean Vanier in 1964 in France and now there are over 100 communities in 29 countries, where about 2,000 people live, including the assistants and those with disabilities. There is no deliberate distinction between the assistants and those who are mentally disabled; all give and all receive. Jean Vanier has often explained that what characterizes L'Arche is the union of the three main aspects of the spiritual, the living together and the professional. Members of L'Arche communities are members of real homes, where they live as families, sharing the daily tasks and being part of the communities and surrounding neighbourhoods.

L'Arche communities have a Christian foundation and most of them, but not all, have a Christian ethos. When L'Arche began in Muslim and Hindu parts of the world, however, Jean Vanier realized that the sufferings of the people were the same and that the need to worship was the same, even though it was through faith paths other than the Christian path. Every person's chosen path of faith is respected in L'Arche. The members of the communities define their individual religious identities and the groups agree on the religious focus of their community houses. The house in Calcutta is an example of a home where the community recognizes all the world faiths. The prayer room has symbols of all the faiths. The members of some of the communities in many countries are of many faiths.

There is the story of Ghadir, a young Muslim girl who was profoundly mentally disabled. She was welcomed into a L'Arche community where she was so trusting in her weakness that she, more than many who had sought to do so through words, was able to create real communion between Christians and Muslims.

When the Third Parliament of Religions took place in Cape Town in celebration of the Millennium, the participants sought to develop friendship and understanding across the faiths. I have touched on the value of this gathering for listening and sharing in Chapter 1. An important piece of work in Cape Town was the publication of a booklet which includes wonderful examples of faith, and interfaith-based practical projects for community building and for human development all over the world. The sections include: building bridges of understanding, meeting essential needs and pursuing universal human rights.[8]

The Fourth Parliament of Religions took place in Barcelona in July 2004. Muslims were strongly represented and they were anxious to dissociate themselves from violence and terrorism. The parliament was an opportunity for Muslims from all over the world to talk and for people of other faiths from all over the world to listen to them. The need for all the religions to work together for peace in the world was an important focus. A lot of concern was expressed about the lack of clean water in the world, and about the challenge this represented to people of faith. The debts of the poor and the care of refugees were also discussed.

No religion has made a greater contribution to gatherings of people of faith, to the building of bridges between the faiths and to work for the future of the world than the Sikh religion. I write about Sikhism in Chapter 6 as a religion that arose in the Punjab as the result of the interaction between Hinduism and Islam, based on the teachings of Guru Nanak. The beliefs of Sikhism may be summed up in the phrase *'One God and one humanity.'* Sikhs are taught to work and fight for what is just and peaceful on every level of life.

The Baha'i faith has also made a great contribution to understanding between the people of the world. Baha'is play an important part in work for justice and peace around the world, including human rights work, women's development and work for racial equality. They attend United Nations meetings and conferences. They have consultative status with the UN Economic and Social Council.

The International Society for Krishna Consciousness (ISKCON), started, and is still the main organization involved in, the very practical 'Food for Life' programme. This work was begun by Swami Srila Prabhupada, who asked his followers not to allow anyone within ten miles of a temple to go without food. The programme is now operating in 60 countries in the world, distributing free vegetarian food, companionship and advice to hungry and needy people. The programme was very active during the floods of Mozambique when whole villages were covered with water and most of the crops destroyed. Many of those involved in this service are young people, members of ISKCON and others of many world faiths working together. Over 400 free meals are provided each day to homeless people in London alone. I have visited an ISKCON community in Leicester and have heard members speak about the programme and about their commitment to it.[9]

All the main world faiths have a concern for ecological issues, peace and the well-being of the human race. A Korean version of the 'Declaration Towards a Global Ethic' moved away from the focus of the main declaration, which was on humanity, and stressed the unity of all life. It stated:

> We have come to believe that the Earth, heaven and all that lives on Earth and all humanity comprise one life-community organically interdependent. Thus we judge that all kinds of oppression,

exploitation and domination are unjust destruction of this life community.[10]

In Leicester there is a shared project between Christians and Hindus for the care and restoration of the Vrindavan area, the legendary birthplace of the Lord Krishna. Vrindavan is 80 miles south of Delhi. By the 1980s most of the trees had been cut down, making the area dusty and unproductive. The Vrindavan Forest Revival Project, in partnership with the World Wildlife Fund, organized a big tree-planting programme with associated educational programmes. The Yamuna River has been cleaned as part of the wider programme. The Vrindavan Declaration is:

> Nature enjoys being enjoyed but reacts furiously to exploitation. Today's situation is caused by our separation from Krishna and his message of commitment. Let us act on his message to play not to exploit.

Reconciliation and peacemaking between people of faith seems an obvious activity, but it is not always easy, and divisions, misunderstandings and wars continue, some of them encouraged and some of them caused by people of faith. I have focused on religion, suffering, strife and warfare in Chapter 4.

What is clear is that if extreme or fanatical religious people are responsible for prejudice, divisions and war, other religious people are the ones who are called to challenge the extremists and to work for transformation and for reconciliation and peacemaking.

In 1994 a conference was held in the Vatican when the theme was 'Healing the World: Religions for Peace'. The conference was organized by the World Conference on Religion and Peace (WCRP) and about 1,000 people from 63 countries attended. The WCRP was founded in 1970 and is international and interfaith. It is dedicated to promoting cooperation among the world's religions and to sharing resources for worldwide peace with justice.[11] At the conference Pope John Paul II gave the opening address when he spoke of the unity of religion and peace. He said, 'To wage war in the name of religion is a blatant contradiction.'

It is encouraging to see that at the conference, when participants from the world faiths discussed their concern for reducing violence and war, the need for respect for human rights, the protection of children and the need for ecological harmony, was followed by the involvement of participants and other members of WCRP in reconciliation and peacemaking all over the world. A good example of their work is seen in what they have done towards peace and understanding between people in Sarajevo.

Paul Knitter, an American theologian, has said that movement and change for a better world may well be from the other direction, beginning with shared action by people of the world faiths. The recognition of the urgent need for shared work for our one suffering world by people of faith may lead to action that is followed by dialogue and understanding. Shared concern and urgent action for the world and its people may then lead to people getting to know each other and on to the development of trust.

My own experience in organizing work camps in the developing world has certainly been that when people recognize a common need and then work together to meet it they do develop trust, no matter how great the differences between them.

The advantage of movement beginning with shared action is that it does not depend upon the religions to challenge their members, but, rather, depends upon the real suffering of the world and its people. The suffering is 'the motivation to stir up a globally recognized need for dialogue'.

Persons from all religious traditions can ... see, feel and respond to the crises facing our Earth. Such recognition can lead to the conclusion that the religions must respond to these crises. A sense of solidarity is an invitation to interaction and conversation.[12]

Paul Knitter's challenge is that the way to begin work with people of the world faiths is not by looking into our own faith but rather by looking straight at the condition of the real world and at the people who suffer in it.

It is the voices of the millions who for the most part stand outside the official precincts of religion and who have not attended the international religious conferences who are calling religious persons together and beckoning them to act and speak together in order to heal the wounds of the world.[13]

Nowhere are the ordinary people asking their faith leaders to work for transformation, healing and peace more than in the Middle East today.

In Chapter 4 I referred to the centuries of persecution faced by the Jewish people at the hands of Christians, including the Holocaust. Some persecution even continues today, including persecution in the UK, and not least in the Middle East. In November 2003 an opinion poll of EU citizens stated that Israel was seen as the greatest danger to world peace. It was as late as 1965, at the Second Vatican Council, that the Roman Catholic Church officially announced that the crucifixion of Christ was not the responsibility of the Jewish people. This declaration has helped in reconciliation. Some theologians have worked to change people's attitudes to Jewish people and to encourage listening and sharing. One important aspect of this work has been the raising of awareness of Jesus as a Jewish person, living in a Jewish culture. Jews have also made efforts recently to portray Christianity in a positive light, some seeing it as God's gift to the Gentile world and encouraging understanding and friendship. The historian Martin Gilbert has published a book on the contribution made by Christians to the rescue of Jewish people during the Holocaust.[14] Those who work for understanding and respect for Jewish people can never relax their efforts, however.

In Britain the development of the Council of Christians and Jews has played an important role in reconciliation. The council was inaugurated in the middle of World War Two in 1942, and aims to fight against all forms of discrimination, prejudice and intolerance, especially anti-Semitism. It also aims to encourage Christians and Jews to respect each other's beliefs and to dig deeply into their common ground.[15]

In the Middle East reconciliation between Jews and Christians is much more complicated because, as I have already noted, the simple acceptance by some Christians, especially those in Britain and America, of the Jewish people's right to the land of Israel, has led to the deprivation and marginalization of the Palestinian people, both Muslim and Christian. Many Muslims and Christians have suffered the loss of their lands and homes and they are still struggling for a secure future.

Many of the Palestinian Christians see their role as go-betweens from their Muslim brothers and sisters to their Jewish neighbours in working for reconciliation.

Afif Safieh is a Greek Orthodox Christian and until recently the Palestinian delegate to the UK. He puts out regular messages and information by e-mail, much of it seeking to build understanding and peace. A spring 2003 message spoke of the work European Jews who are members of peace groups are doing towards peace, including the demand for an end to the occupation of Palestinian lands by the Israeli government and the withdrawal of the Israeli settlers from the occupied areas. They further called for security for both Israel and Palestine and for the right of both states to have Jerusalem as their capital.

There are many Jewish people who are working for peace with justice in the Middle East. Some Jews have even said that they see Zionism as a rebellion against God, showing lack of concern for all the other people of God in the Middle Eastern region. Mark Ellis, an American Jewish theologian, writes about the strong sense of justice and community at the heart of Judaism and challenges Israeli Jews to be just in their dealings with the Palestinian people.[16]

Jeff Halper runs the Israeli Committee Against House Demolitions.[17] He was especially vocal when a young volunteer, Rachel Corrie, was killed by the Israeli army whilst protesting against the house demolitions in Gaza in 2003. He saw her as representing the many people who are killed when the army demolishes houses. He constantly raises awareness all over the world of the suffering caused by house demolitions, and appeals to Israel to end this cruel practice. He works hard and offers suggestions, including new political models, for a positive way forward for Palestinian and Israeli people. His commitment and bravery are very encouraging and bring hope to people who are often traumatized. He has said:

> We, members of the Israeli peace camp, resist demolition as Rachel did, to block the bulldozers with our bodies, and to rebuild Palestinian homes when they are demolished. For by doing so we, as Israeli Jews, are saying to the Palestinians, 'We acknowledge your existence as people and your right to be in this country. We want to share this country with you, based on the rights of both our peoples. We seek a common future based on a just peace. We refuse to be enemies.'[18]

Bishop Riah abu el Assal, the Anglican Bishop of Jerusalem, challenges Christians, Jews and Muslims to meet regularly and to present themselves as 'instruments of reconciliation'.

Father Elias Chacour is a Melkite priest. As a child he lived in a beautiful Palestinian village where the people, including his own family, lived peacefully with their Jewish neighbours. In 1947, as Israel came to birth, the village, along with many others, was destroyed and the people became refugees. Elias Chacour has spent his life in work for new understanding between the Jewish, Christian and Muslim people of the region.[19] He came to England in June 2003 and I heard him speak on the complications of the Middle Eastern situation, where no one is safe. He said, 'Our life has been turned into a funeral procession on both sides.' He pointed out that peace involves the acceptance by people of faith in the region of each other, not the hiding of differences. He said, 'I was a child, created in the image of God. The soldiers who destroyed our house were also born in the image of God.'

He appealed for friendship for all the people of the region, who do not need money or weapons, but love and solidarity. He said, 'Please take our side and help us to understand the Jews. Do not think you are helping us by working against the Jews. We need a future for all the children.' Elias Chacour has developed a secondary school in Ibillin in Galilee where there are some Jewish teachers for the Palestinian students. The school is a shining example of hope for education and a shared future for all the people of the region. When 16 Jewish people were killed, 300 of the Palestinian students gave blood for the injured, out of a total of 350 students. Permission has been given by the Israeli government for a Palestinian university to be developed, and this is now being established.

The hope for a peaceful future in the Middle East lies in the work of people of all the faiths there, Christian, Jewish and Muslim. It is vital that those working for peace and justice overcome the extremists of all faiths. There are many signs of hope, in the shared peace vigils, the rebuilding of demolished homes, the shared tree planting and the dismantling of blockades. There are the mass rallies organized by the Coalition of Women for a Just Peace, and the gatherings of the interfaith women's groups.

There is the work of both Israeli and Palestinian groups for the health of the people.

On New Year's Eve 2001 there was a march for justice and peace from Bethlehem to Jerusalem, which was shared by the church leaders in the Holy Land with Muslims and Jews. People from all the faiths and from all over the world joined together in the walk. The marchers called for an end to the occupation of the Palestinian West Bank, for the opening up of Jerusalem to people of all the faiths and for people of faith to pray together.

The marchers had only walked for one mile when Israeli armoured vehicles blocked the road. The church leaders walked forward, on to the guns, offered olive branches to the soldiers and asked to be allowed to continue the walk. They were allowed to go on as far as the checkpoint between Bethlehem and Jerusalem, but not into Jerusalem itself. An act of worship by people of all the faiths was held at the checkpoint and later they all gathered at the Pool of Bethesda and made a further call for peace and healing.

At New Year 2002 the Muslim, Jewish and Christian leaders met at Alexandria. They had the backing of the Israeli and Palestinian leaders as they called for peace and formed a permanent committee to work for peace. The Alexandria Declaration is:

In the name of God who is Almighty, Merciful and Compassionate, we, who have gathered as religious leaders from the Muslim, Christian and Jewish communities, pray for true peace in Jerusalem and the Holy Land and declare our commitment to ending the violence and bloodshed that denies the right to life and dignity.

According to our faith traditions, killing innocents in the name of God is a desecration of his Holy Name, and defames religion in the world. The violence in the Holy Land is an evil which must be opposed by all people of good faith. We seek to live together as neighbours, respecting the integrity of each other's historical and religious inheritance. We call upon all to oppose incitement, hatred and the misrepresentation of the other.[20]

I have many links of friendship with Jewish people in the UK and the Middle East and with Palestinian Christians. I also have Muslim friends in the Middle East, the UK and around the world.

I have touched on the fear Muslims have of the western media, especially after 9/11. Many Muslims feel that they never have a fair hearing. The report of the Runnymede Trust, *Islamophobia, a challenge for Us All*, which I have looked at in Chapter 4, was published as late as 1997.

The long history of relations between Christians and Muslims, and the fact that both their religions see evangelism of those outside as vitally important, have contributed to the guardedness with which they approach each other. There are, however, many opportunities for them to get to know each other, and I have introduced some of these in Chapter 1. If the barriers and ignorance can be overcome then the fear may also be overcome and people may work together.

It is also possible that an urgent situation may compel people to come together in action for change and healing. Many members of councils of faith throughout the UK have been at pains to publicize the horror their Muslim members have felt at the atrocities committed on September 11th 2001. Councils of faith have also been the vehicles for Muslims themselves to express their rejection and condemnation of terrorism. Muslims have also invited their friends of other faiths to join them in prayer vigils for peace, and many of these have been held. Dr Ataullah Siddique, from the Markfield Islamic Institute and a member of the Leicester Council of Faiths, has said that he is very disturbed by the bunching together of all Muslims as violent criminals. He has said that Muslims are very keen to condemn violence and to have their voices heard. The problem is that it is hard to get the media to listen to the peaceful Muslim voices, let alone to promote them. Ibrahim Mogra, a Muslim leader and teacher in Leicester, has said, 'I do not know what we can do to convince the media and the general public that we are against terrorism, and that Islam is against the taking of innocent life.'

In September 2002 the Muslim Council of Great Britain published *The Quest for Sanity: Reflections on September 11th and the Aftermath*. In a letter recommending the book the Secretary General of the Council, Iqbal Sacranie, wrote, 'We urge you ... to stand firmly for truth and justice.' The book begins with quotations from the Qu'ran.

> Verily, God commands justice and
> the doing of good, and liberality to kin, and
> He forbids all shameful and evil deeds, and
>   oppression.
> He instructs you, that perchance you may take
>   heed.[21]

The Quest for Sanity condemns the September 11th atrocity without hesitation. There is a chapter that includes condemnation of the atrocity by Muslim scholars from all over the world. In his foreword to the book Iqbal Sacranie writes:

> What happened on September 11th, 2001 was simply
> evil and criminal ... Terrorism has no religion. Its
> aim is to spread enmity and destruction throughout

civilized societies ... Islam places a unilateral obligation on Muslims towards the welfare of their fellow human beings and the societies in which they live and to work for the common good of all.[22]

This book has been published out of the desperation of many British Muslims to communicate with the non-Muslims in the UK and to help them to understand that they are peaceful and God-fearing people who would never commit the atrocity of September 11th 2001 or any of the other atrocities of recent years. The book is also written for members of the Muslim community and asks them not to listen to those who would advocate violence.

The book is an important bridge-building exercise between the Muslim community in the UK, the people of the other faiths and the wider community. Many bridges are being built between Muslims and their neighbours of other faiths in Britain today. Friendship is leading to participation in community projects.

As women's interfaith groups grow in popularity it is increasingly possible for women of other faiths to speak up for their Muslim friends, especially when they are misrepresented as downtrodden and ignored by Muslim men. The story of Muslim and Christian women working together to bring peace in Bradford, during and after the riots of 1995, is encouraging.[23]

The hostility that has flared up between Hindus and Muslims in India has led to Christians and Muslims working together there to protect each other and to challenge the Hindu majority to be tolerant. The Anglican Bishop of Calcutta has initiated gatherings and shared work by Hindu, Muslim and Christian people in response to the troubles the country is facing. I have explored some of the issues surrounding the situation in India in Chapter 4, including the recent changes since the May 2004 elections. The victory for the inclusive Congress Party is a wonderful sign of hope.

The situation in India has affected relations between Hindus and Muslims in the UK. The Inter Faith Network for the UK, established in 1987 to foster respect and good relations between the faith communities at national and local levels, has found that it has had to be very sensitive to tensions between Muslims and Hindus on the Indian subcontinent, for these can soon have repercussions on otherwise harmonious faith relationships in Britain.

It is easy for Hindus to promote their faith as having a great contribution to make to peacemaking and unity in the world. Yoga arose within Hinduism and means 'to join' or 'that which unites'. It is a challenge to people of faith to unite within the self, with others, with the environment, with the universal and with God.

One famous Hindu who built a bridge of understanding between Hinduism and the people of the other faiths was Vivekananda, disciple of Ramakrishna, whom I have introduced as attending and speaking at the first World Parliament of Religions in Chicago. He appealed for people to work hard for understanding between the faiths and for them to link their meditation with their service to the world. Gandhi was another Hindu who worked for peace and understanding between the religions. He founded ashram communities where people of all faiths were welcome, and where the practical work led on to understanding and to work for peace and justice in the world.

Gandhi found common ground in the lives and teachings of Jesus Christ and the Lord Buddha. The life of the Buddha was a life lived from the realization that the individual could never reach peace and enlightenment by ignoring the world, but, rather, had to go through the suffering world, bringing unity and peace wherever possible. One of the challenges of Buddhism is to see conflict in the world as the opportunity for peacemaking, by living peacefully, through the eightfold path, by developing detachment, wisdom and compassion, and by going to the roots of conflict.

Sri Lanka is one of the main homes of Theravada or Orthodox Buddhism: 70 per cent of the people are Sinhala Buddhists. I have described some of the struggles of Sri Lanka in Chapter 4. Many people of faith have worked for peace with justice and are currently enjoying a more peaceful period since the agreement on a ceasefire was signed in February 2002. However, this peaceful period has been threatened by quarrels between the President and the Prime Minister and, most severely, by the killing in August 2005 of the Foreign Minister, a Tamil who had always worked with the government. Many of the Buddhists have worked with Christians, Hindus and Muslims towards the hoped-for peace.

The World Solidarity Forum is an example of an inter-faith body, founded in Thailand in 1990, with members from 19 countries, which has worked for peace with justice in Sri Lanka. It includes members of the four main religions of the country, who are also from the three main ethnic communities. It has organized a regular programme of study, dialogue and action, including public demonstrations, peace walks, house-to-house visiting and public campaigning for peace. Some of the visits and walks have been to refugee camps to meet those who have suffered most from the war. The statement of 'Samadana Pradakshinawa' or 'sharing peace on the streets' was signed by people of the faiths in Sri Lanka and the UK in March 2002. The challenge is one of 'taking to the streets in a movement for peace on the basis of justice for all sections of the people'. Samadana Pradakshinawa is being taken up by many people of faith.

Rissho Kosei-kai was founded in Japan in 1938 as an organization that would work to fulfil the Buddha's wish for world peace and the happiness of humanity. It now has 239 branches in Japan and 6 other branches all over the world. All the peace work is grounded in the Lotus Sutra which the members read every morning and evening. The members focus on becoming *bodhisattvas*, those who seek the truth and then work in the world to share that truth and compassion with others. They support a wide range of peace projects, medical work, education and vocational training. They work to help refugees and the poorest of the poor around the world.

Nichidatsu Fuji was a Japanese Buddhist and a disciple of Gandhi who devoted his life to peace and justice while living through World War Two, the Holocaust and the bombing of Hiroshima and Nagasaki. He worked for peace and unity in the world by founding the Nipponzan Myohoji Buddhist order and by making a worldwide pilgrimage for peace, during which he built peace pagodas.

The idea of the peace pagodas went back about 2,600 years to the first stupas that enshrined the relics of the Lord Buddha, to be revered throughout time. The pagodas are dedicated as a sign of the possibility of universal peace on the Earth. They are symbolic of light in the darkness of the present-day world, a visible and tangible appeal that may awaken the people of the Earth to work for peace with justice. It has been said that as one views a peace pagoda it appears to rise up as an invocation from the earth, water, air and sky. People of all faiths may appreciate the plea of the pagoda to them to work for the sacredness of life, for peace and justice. 'The vision of a pagoda has the power to bring about a spiritual transformation. It illumines the dawn of a spiritual civilization.'[24]

Nichidatsu Fuji built his first peace pagoda in Japan after the bombing of Hiroshima and Nagasaki, believing that the horrors of the war would arouse the feelings of the people of the world for peace.

The members of the order continue to build peace pagodas and to walk for peace all over the world. As they walk they beat drums and chant the prayer for peace,

'Na-mu Myo-Ho-Ren-Ge-Kyo', a sacred prayer from the Lotus Sutra.

In 1994 there was a pilgrimage from Auschwitz to Hiroshima and 3,000 miles of the journey were on foot. The Revd Gyoshu Sasamori said of the pilgrimage:

> We started our journey at one of the most tragic places of the war ... we ended it at the place where the first atomic bomb was dropped on human beings ... We offered prayers for the victims of all wars. We heard the voices of the victims in our hearts ... we can establish new values today and for the future.[25]

A Buddhist woman who has put the wisdom of her faith into practice in a situation of suffering and strife is Aung San Suu Kyi. She was placed under house arrest in Burma in 1989 for challenging the military dictatorship there. Her National League for Democracy won the 1990 elections, but the military government refused to stand down. Aung San Suu Kyi was awarded the Nobel Peace Prize in 1991 and released from house arrest in 1995, though her life remained very restricted. She was arrested in 2003 and imprisoned in Insein Prison in Rangoon, causing great anxiety to her supporters in Burma and around the world. On her release from prison she was again put under house arrest. Her struggle for peace and unity continues but there seems to be no end to the determination of the military regime to stay in power and to exclude her. They continue to arrest and imprison people who oppose them and to use forced labour.

An insight into Aung San Suu Kyi's Buddhist values was presented by her late husband at the Pope Paul VI Memorial Lecture in 1997. Her definition of development is spiritual development and not material development. Any development must put people and their human rights first. Spiritual development is enabled by the four 'heavenly abodes' of Buddhism: loving kindness, compassion, sympathetic joy and equanimity. Work for development and justice can never be motivated by anger but must always be motivated by love and compassion balanced by wisdom.[26]

The Tibetan people now living in India and other parts of the world since they were driven from Tibet in 1950 have survived without bitterness because they have remained loyal to their Buddhist faith and culture, motivated by love and compassion for all, especially for the children of the world. There are 18 excellent Tibetan children's villages in India. Three monasteries destroyed in Tibet have been rebuilt. The head of Tibetan Buddhism, the Dalai Lama, has always been clear that it is outlook on life, on religions and on the world that is the key to the future of the world. He has said:

> Conflicts and crises arise in the name of different religious traditions ... the most effective method to overcome these conflicts is close contact and an exchange among those of various beliefs, not only on an intellectual level, but in deeper spiritual experiences ... the purpose of all the major religious traditions is not to construct big temples on the outside but to create temples of goodness and compassion on the inside, in our hearts ... Every major religion has the potential to create this.[27]

The Dalai Lama is in himself a shining example of someone who has faith and hope for his people and for the world, when everything that has happened to him, including his expulsion from Tibet and his exile and failed efforts to negotiate with the government of China, might have led to resignation and even despair. In Chapter 2 I suggested that he is a fine example of a whole and holy person. The way he spoke out following the Tiananmen Square atrocity in 1989 was typical. He said that 'the brave students and their supporters showed the Chinese leadership and the world the human face of that great race'.[28] In 1994 he gave the John Main Seminar in London when he spoke on chapter 5 of Matthew's Gospel, 'Love your enemies and pray for your persecutors.' He referred to a Mahayana Buddhist text, *The Compendium of Practices*, in which Shantideva asks, 'If you do not practise compassion towards your enemy towards whom can you practise it?' He also introduced *A Guide to the Bodhisattva's Way of Life*, stressing that it is vital to work to develop a right attitude towards an enemy. He went on to develop the idea that an enemy may be the best spiritual teacher, because listening will provide the opportunity for the development of tolerance, patience and understanding. This listening may lead on to the development of compassion and even altruism, equanimity and calmness.

The Dalai Lama's approach to work for reconciliation, peace and justice in the world is comparable with other approaches, religious and secular. The Quaker approach, in which the reconciler struggles to get people, on an individual, group, national or international level, to see each other's point of view as the beginning of breaking down barriers is the same as that of the Dalai Lama. Adam Curle worked as a Quaker reconciler for 40 years and has written about how difficult he found it to get people to even listen to anything good of the opposition.[29] He worked at building relationships with and between people and thus creating the trust within which the truth could be spoken and even occasionally heard. He accepts that work for reconciliation does not in his experience lead directly to peace, but it does have an influence once peace has been declared. He also confesses that in many current situations of violence the peace-maker can normally do nothing to work with vain and self-serving people who are committing violence, and can only hope to find people who want peace and to work with them to change the climate in a region from fear to hope.

The Quaker approach to reconciliation work, leading to the building of a unified and peaceful world, should be representative of the approach of all Christians. The incarnation of God as a human being is central to the faith and life of Christians. It is a model for bridge-building between heaven and earth and between peoples, all with the light of God in them. It is a challenge to every member of the faith. A wonderful example of bridge-building in recent history was the work of Desmond Tutu and the Truth and Reconciliation Commission that was set up when apartheid ended in South Africa. The work of the commission did lead to the truth of many atrocities being told and to some healing between former enemies.[30]

Christians in the UK, and I have explored this in Chapter 1, have a special responsibility to build bridges of understanding between themselves and all the other people who live around them, including, and perhaps especially, the people of faith. This is pioneering and vital work, but most of the time it is not dangerous.

There are Christians who live in dangerous situations who also work for peace between themselves and people of other faiths, including the Christians of Egypt. The Coptic Christians, included in my introduction, are tackling opposition to them and their faith by simple living in the land of their ancestors and by offering service to those of the Muslim faith around them. This is also the approach of Christians in Pakistan, where the churches offer education and health care to whole communities, mostly the Muslim people. Christians in Japan are a wonderful example of people who have been persecuted in the past and who now live with faith in a natural way, working hard as ordinary members of their country and communities and serving others whenever the need arises. Currently they are working to help people of Korean origin who have been marginalized in their communities. They are also building bridges with the people of Korea and other surrounding Asian countries.

The 'Declaration Towards a Global Ethic' is an uplifting reminder of the recent commitment of people of faith to transformation, reconciliation, peace and justice in the world, but it is also a reminder that most of the difficult work still remains to be done. The hope is that people of faith will be those who, aware of their responsibility for one another and for the planet, will never give up the struggle, shared when possible, for a united, just and peaceful world.

The hope is, further, that people of faith will never forget the challenge of Mahatma Gandhi, to recall the face of the poorest and most helpless person they have ever seen and to ask if the action they take will be of any use to him.

6

Short outlines of the world faiths

The subject of the world faiths is vast. As I have explained in my introduction, I write this book as a Christian. I have chosen to refer to the eight other major historic world faiths, five of which, Hinduism, Judaism, Buddhism, Islam and Sikhism, are well represented in Britain. The three other faiths, Zoroastrianism, Jainism and the Baha'i faith, are also present in Britain. Their members are small in numbers but they play an important part in society and in interfaith organizations and work.

The 2001 census was the first in the UK to include an optional question about religion.

- About four million people refused to answer the question.
- In England and Wales 37.3 million people, 71.7 per cent of the total population, described themselves as Christian. Over the UK as a whole 42,079,417 people said they were Christian.
- A total of 1.5 million people, 3 per cent, described themselves as Muslim in England and Wales, while there were 1,591,126 Muslims in the UK.
- There were 552,000, 1.1 per cent, Hindus in England and Wales and 558,810 in the UK.
- There were 329,000, 0.6 per cent, Sikhs in England and Wales and 336,149 in the UK.
- There were 260,000, 0.5 per cent, Jewish people in England and Wales, and 266,740 in the UK.
- There were 144,000, 0.3 per cent, Buddhists in England and Wales, and 151,816 in the UK.
- There were also 7.7 million people, 14.8 per cent, who said either that they had no religion or that they followed a religion not recognized in the survey. This

figure included the 390,000 people who hit the headlines by identifying themselves as Jedi.

There are many ways of looking at the census figures. Many members of the Christian Churches have pointed out that, according to the figures, Britain is still a Christian country and that we may have to look for ways of working with Christians who no longer attend Christian worship on a regular basis. Others would say that the numbers of people of other faiths are small but very significant. This significance is heightened because people of other faiths tend to live in the larger cities, where they make up very important sections of the communities and a larger percentage is religiously active, either at home or at the public place of worship, including temple, mosque or gurdwara.

Leicester, for example, is the city-wide authority with the largest proportion of non-white people, mainly made up of its Asian/Hindu population which is currently one third of the city's overall population and is growing.

Iqbal Sacranie, Secretary General of the Muslim Council of Britain, said of the census results:

> Up to now, Muslims have been statistically invisible, and thus easily marginaliszed. The census output is a strong signal to central and local government, social services and employers that the needs of all sections of Britain's multicultural society must be fairly and equitably addressed.[1]

I believe that the majority Christian community has a responsibility not only to learn about and meet members of the other faiths in the UK and beyond, but also to support and work for justice and recognition for them.

Eight very short presentations of the world faiths other than the Christian faith follow. It is of course impossible in such brief descriptions to do justice to the diversity of faith and practice within these traditions. The hope is that readers will move on from these short studies to meet the people of faith and to read about the faiths, including the books in the resource section. The introductions are in the order of the emergence of the faiths, beginning with Zoroastrianism and ending with the Baha'i faith.

Zoroastrianism

The Zoroastrian world population today is approximately 150,000, with 40,000 in Iran and about 75,000 in India. The others live in the USA, Canada and Britain. There are about 5 – 6,000 in Britain.[2]

Zoroastrianism is perhaps the most ancient of the great world religions. Zarathushtra, probably the first great priest and prophet, is thought to have lived in the north-east of present-day Iran, near to the border with Afghanistan, around 1500 to 1200 BCE. He experienced a series of divine revelations and was inspired to preach a new message, for which he was persecuted, until after many years a local king in the north east accepted it and from there it spread.

By the time of the great Persian Empire in the sixth century BCE Zoroastrianism was the official religion of the area from northern India to Greece and Egypt. Other faiths were encouraged at this time, which lasted until the conquest by Alexander the Great in the fourth century BCE. Ups and downs followed until the seventh-century rise of Islam when many of the Zoroastrians retreated to the desert and then to India. In India they mainly live in the area around Mumbai, where they are known as the Parsis, the people from Pars or Persia. More Zoroastrians left the land of their origin when the Ayatollah Khomeini established the Islamic Republic there in 1979.

The Zoroastrian prayer texts are known as the Avesta. The Gathas are thought to include Zarathushtra's own words and are therefore the most central texts. They were written in the ninth and tenth centuries in the common era; they systematize the teachings of Zarathushtra.

Zarathushtra or Zoroaster called for the worship of the one good creator God, to be through the medium of fire. The energy of God is represented by fire or by the sun. Zoroastrians pray in front of the sun, a candle or other light. In places of worship a fire is kept constantly alight.

Zarathushtra called for all people to live in harmony through making wise choices in life and through mutual respect. He taught that every person was a divine creation, destined to work with God and to be with God. He taught that each person should seek a balance of the spiritual and the material, of soul and body. Marriage and the nurturing of children were necessary, as was a love and care for God's good creation, the world and the natural environment. The spread of goodness and happiness in a joyous and light-filled world, together with the fighting of evil, is the lifelong challenge to the people of the faith.

Each person will face two judgements, of spirit and of body, and the whole person will thus finally be raised to union with God. Zarathushtra saw good and evil as realities in the conscience, with the free choice of good, from the one true God and from 'bounteous immortals', leading to happiness for oneself and for others. He saw the world as basically good, but envisaged a battle with evil following which good would triumph. The free choice of evil, including violence, chaos and the will to destroy, emanating from the independent and destructive spirit, will lead to unhappiness, struggle and war.

Zoroastrianism is a small religion but it is increasingly practised in community, especially by its younger members all over the world. There are many classes and meetings for worship and the celebration of festivals.

Zoroastrianism is very ancient and is recognized as having made a contribution to the development of other world religions. It calls its followers, who have free will, to the worship of the one God and to the struggle for good and against evil. Its followers believe in the resurrection of the body and the last judgement. Zoroastrianism is often seen as a bridge between religions, particularly between Hinduism and Buddhism and Judaism, Christianity and Islam.

Judaism

The Jewish world population today is about 14,434,000. The population of Jewish people in Israel is 6,145,000. In the USA the Jewish population is 5,880,000. In Britain the Jewish population is approximately 285,000. This small population is largely due to people going to live in Israel in the twentieth century but also to the growing trend of young men to marry out of the faith. London has the largest Jewish community of any European city apart from Paris. There are also strong communities in Manchester, Leeds, Brighton and Glasgow.

Judaism began as a nomadic religion, initially with Abraham who journeyed with God, and then with Moses who led the Exodus for the freedom of the people. After Moses' death the Ark of the Covenant was carried on, finally to Jerusalem. In the sixth century BCE, after the destruction of Solomon's temple, the Jews were exiled to Babylon. Seventy years later Cyrus the Great of Persia captured Babylon and allowed the Jews to return to Jerusalem. They made their pilgrimage back to their homeland and the temple was rebuilt.

In the new community around Jerusalem there was a strict separation between Jewish people and everyone else. The Jewish community practised circumcision; observance of the Sabbath, from Friday evening to Saturday evening; the recognition of the law of Moses, the Torah; and the observation of the temple rituals. Marriage was arranged strictly within the community. There was only one place of sacrifice, the temple, and gradually, even before the temple was destroyed in 70 CE by the Romans, there was the need to set up synagogues for teaching and worship for the people who lived too far away to visit Jerusalem. Gradually Jewish communities grew up in many areas and cultural differences also grew.

Judea came under the Roman Empire from 63 BCE until 200 CE following a long period of ups and downs, attacks, revolts and sufferings. In 66 CE the Jewish community revolted, leading to a devastating defeat, the capture of Jerusalem by Rome and the destruction of the temple in 70 CE. The diaspora that followed this destruction of the last temple continued until the formation of the state of Israel in 1948. The communities were linked together a little through the emergence of teachers or rabbis, and through adherence to the calendar, the festivals, and loyalty to the communities. This long period of exile was a time of great contrasts for the people; it included periods of intellectual flowering, the writing of stories and prayers, and also periods of horrific persecution, including persecution by Christians, not least at the time of the crusades.

When the Jews dispersed after destruction of the temple in 70 CE they moved to the north and the west, forming two main cultural groups, the Ashkenazi Jews, who trace their roots back to eastern Europe, and the Sephardi Jews, who trace their roots to Spain and north Africa. The majority of British Orthodox Jews come from the Ashkenazi cultural background.

The Jewish people recognize God as transcendent and also immanent, the good creator who is obeyed through keeping his law, contained in the Torah, throughout life. The Torah is the first five books of the Hebrew Bible. The other books of the Hebrew Bible are also central to Jewish life, together with the originally oral Talmud, which is a huge compendium including the writings of rabbis over many years.

The Jewish Reform movement began in Germany and spread from there. The West London Synagogue was opened in 1842 and in 1972 the first woman rabbi was ordained. Liberal Judaism began early in the twentieth century and the St John's Wood synagogue became the centre from which it has spread.

The differences between the Jewish communities are most likely to be about what constitutes the community, ways of worship, general behaviour, what it means to be the 'chosen people of God', and how the land of Israel is seen. In terms of actual belief the main difference is that Orthodox Jews believe that the word of God in both its written and its oral form is directly revealed by God. Non-Orthodox Jews hold that the oral Torah may be revised and adapted to modern life.

Hinduism

There are an estimated 900 million Hindus worldwide with 720 million of them in India where they are about 80 per cent of the population. There are 600,000 Hindus in Britain.

'Hindu' comes from 'Sindhu' which is the Persian name for the River Indus. The Aryan people moved into the Indus Valley area around 1500 BCE. The Persians called the people 'the people beyond the Sindhu', or 'Hindu'. The word 'Hindu' originally meant Indian and gradually came to describe the religion.

G. Tilak, a late nineteenth-century nationalist reformer, said that what made one a Hindu included acceptance of the Vedas with reverence; recognition of the fact that the means or ways to salvation are diverse; and the realization of the truth that the number of gods to be worshipped is large. Gandhi always said that his people's religion was evolutionary, a living organism which was liable to growth and to decay. He saw his faith as like a huge tree, with one root but innumerable branches.

Most of Britain's 600,000 Hindus came to this country after the World War Two. At first they were mainly men seeking work, who were later joined by friends and then by their families. A large Hindu community moved to Britain in the early 1970s. A few came from Kenya and Tanzania and the majority from Uganda, following persecution there. The largest British Hindu community today is in Leicester, where it is approximately 25 per cent of the total population. There are also large communities in London, Coventry, Birmingham and Leeds.

The Hindu religion is based on right conduct in every aspect of life. *Sanatana dharma* is good order throughout the universe; action in life is therefore placed in the perspective of the eternal. For most but not all Hindus this is lived out on Earth within the limitations of the caste system. Each Hindu is born into a caste, a social group with its own duties and place in a hierarchy of the castes. Most Hindus still marry within their caste though many now meet, mix and work with people of all castes or none. All Hindus have great freedom in faith and in worship. They enjoy a whole range of sacred texts and there are millions of religious practices and deities.

The scriptures are divided into those not composed by anyone but directly heard – the eternal sound, heard by the ancients – and those remembered. The *Vedas* and *Upanishads* are said to be divinely revealed and heard; they are chanted in Sanskrit during important ceremonies. The epics, including the *Mahabharata* and the *Ramayana*, are the remembered stories and are very popular. The *Mahabharata* includes the *Bhagavad Gita* or 'Song of the Lord' in which the Lord Krishna teaches the warrior Arjuna about duty and about how to achieve liberation not only from repeated rebirth but from all inner bondage.

God is understood in more philosophical Hindu thought as the one ultimate reality, the Brahman. Sometimes the one God is seen as a trinity, with Brahma representing creation, Vishnu representing preservation and Shiva representing destruction. Hindus aim for *moksha*, to become free from the cycle of births and deaths and rebirths, and to achieve unity with the one supreme God.

Different schools of philosophy have emerged in Hinduism, which lead to different understandings of how unity with God may be achieved. Advaita, or the non-dualistic school, teaches that there is a unity of all things, the Earth, the people and the one supreme God. The spiritual quest is thus towards understanding and experiencing this unity. There is also a school which recognizes that there is ultimate unity between God and the creation, but that there is also difference, giving each person individuality. A third school teaches that God is completely separate from his creation and that unity implies a relationship which is achieved through the spiritual path.

There are countless sacred stories, with Hindu festivals throughout the year. Divali is a well-known festival, the five-day festival of lights. The people remember the story of Rama and Sita returning to Ayodhya and being welcomed by rows of lights after being banished for 14 years during which the evil king Ravana was overcome. The festival is a symbol of light over darkness, of the triumph of good over evil. There is also a focus on Lakshmi, the goddess of good fortune, who visits and blesses homes. This is also the time when business people pay off all their debts and close their accounts. There is the tradition of the accounts being brought to the temple. The day after Divali is the new year of new beginnings and hopes.

Every important point in life and death is marked by ceremony for the Hindu. The stages of life are highlighted, so that seekers are very aware of moving from one stage to another.

Pilgrimage is central to Hindu life and the pilgrim is seen as like the lotus flower, moving from the mud into the light and thus becoming beautiful. The journey inwards is well developed through meditation. Yoga, or union with oneself, with other people and creatures and with God, is the goal for more informed seekers. An important aspect of any pilgrimage is devotion to God, and this has led to the creation of many wonderful songs and poems.

The pilgrim places are obvious and many in India, and include natural features of the landscape, rivers and places special to particular people or deities. One example of a pilgrim place, which I have visited, is Puri on the coast of Orissa, which is sacred as the place of pilgrimage to the Lord Jagganath. The tradition is that Lord Jagganath was a tribal deity who was taken over by Hinduism as an image of Lord Krishna. The stone temple of Puri was built in the twelfth century CE. Every August the Lord Jagganath goes on procession round Puri watched by many thousands of pilgrims.

Buddhism

There are about 360,000,000 Buddhists worldwide. There are approximately 130,000 Buddhists in Britain today.

Buddhism began in the sixth and fifth centuries BCE with the enlightenment of Gotama, who thus became 'Sakyamuni', the *muni*, or sage, of the Sakya clan. He had been born as Prince Siddhartha in about 567 BCE in Kapilavatthu at the foot of the Himalaya mountains. He was born into an aristocratic family and, because sages predicted that he would be either a world renouncer or a ruler, he was protected from pain, suffering and poverty. He married and a son was born. One day he went out and saw suffering, sickness and death. He also met a holy man. Soon after this he became a wanderer, a searcher after religious truth. He tried asceticism but realized that this was not the right way. After many days of meditation, on a full moon night in May, as he was sitting under a Bodhi tree, he realized the truths he later taught, and thus became enlightened. He was 35 years old and for the next 45 years he preached and taught, sharing his experiences in reaching enlightenment. Thus his teaching, *dharma*, grew and became the bedrock of Buddhism, 'Buddha Dharma'.

At the centre of Buddha's answer to the question of suffering was the inevitable process of cause and effect through which everything is linked. He identified the cause of suffering as desire prompted by greed, hatred and ignorance. Ignorance is not seeing that human existence is characterized by impermanence, suffering and the lack of anything unchanging in the person. It is necessary to move from selfishness to selflessness.

This teaching is encapsulated in the Four Noble Truths.

- First, the truth of suffering, *dukkha*, includes intrinsic suffering, the suffering due to impermanence, and the suffering that is inseparable from conditionality.

- Second, the truth of the origin of suffering is craving or thirst for sensual pleasures, craving for existence or non-existence, manifested as ignorance, aversion, attraction, jealousy/envy and pride.

- The third truth is that suffering has an end.

- Fourth, the eightfold path is the path to the end of suffering. The eightfold path is right understanding, right thought, right speech, right action, right livelihood, right effort, right mindfulness, right concentration. Right mindfulness and right concentration are developed through meditation.

The Buddha himself wrote nothing and his teachings were at first memorized and recited in groups and thus handed down orally. According to tradition the scriptures were written down in the first century BCE. They are divided into three main sections or three 'baskets': the teachings of the Buddha, the *sutras*, the writings on the structure and discipline of the monastic life, the *vinaya* texts, and the *abhidharma* or the view of world from the enlightened. The scriptures have always transmitted through the *Sangha* and written down in local languages, one of the earliest and best known being the 'Pali Canon'.

There are two main schools of Buddhism. Theravada Buddhism – the traditional, orthodox Buddhism – is practised in Sri Lanka, Thailand, Cambodia and Burma. Mahayana Buddhism is a more inclusive and very varied form of Buddhism, which is practiced in China, Korea, Japan, Vietnam, and in Tibet, where a distinctive Buddhism has developed. The world-famous Dalai Lama, now living in exile in India, is the head of the Tibetan Buddhists.

In Theravada Buddhism, the ceremonies end with participants taking the five precepts, abstaining from: harming living beings, taking what is not given, false speech, sexual misconduct, and using anything that will damage the mind. They practise the positive qualities of loving kindness, generosity and compassion.

The *Sangha* or community is at the heart of Buddhism. It grew from the five ascetics the Buddha preached to when he first achieved enlightenment. In Theravada Buddhism it is monastic; the monks and nuns practise celibacy and live in monasteries and temples, depending upon the laity for support. In Mahayana Buddhism there are many models of community: for instance, monks marry in some traditions. The community may also be much wider, including the community of the practitioners.

All Buddhists look forward to liberation, when greed, hatred and ignorance have been defeated and when 'nirvana' or the highest bliss is reached. Some Buddhists in the Mahayana traditions believe that there have been many Buddhas. They are those who have reached the state of perfect wisdom and compassion through their lives of service and sacrifice, often in their great compassion opting to return to the world of suffering in order to help others. They are known as *bodhisattvas*.

151

In 1989 the International Network of Engaged Buddhists was formed and its members focused on the creation of a better world in the here and now. They are inspired by the concern of all Buddhists for the elimination of suffering, by their understanding that all is connected, and by their observation that much suffering arises from injustice and greed. One example of an engaged Buddhist group in the UK is the Amida Trust which is inspired by the Pure Land tradition of Japan to work for a pure land in this world. Engaged Buddhists see meditation and work for justice as mutually essential.

Jainism

There are about 4,218,000 Jains in the world, mostly in western India. There are between 25,000 and 30,000 Jains in Britain. They came either directly from India, where their main home is in Gujarat, or, in the 1960s and 1970s, from East Africa.

The largest Jain communities in Britain are in Leicester and London. The Jain Centre in Leicester was designed to appeal to both eastern and western tastes. It includes the life of Mahavira in beautiful stained-glass windows and it attracts visitors from all over the world.

Jainism emerged in the sixth century BCE through the witness of Mahavira, who spent much of his life as a wandering teacher and ascetic, mostly in what is now Bihar. He was the last of 24 *tirthankaras* or bridge-builders, who became enlightened and were removed from the cycle of reincarnation. He was a contemporary of the Buddha. He shared his experiences and insights and promised a way of liberation to all, irrespective of caste, social status or gender. Jains follow Mahavira in self-purification through austerity and fasting. They practise non-violence or *ahimsa*, which means that they seek to cause no harm to any living thing. The three jewels of the faith are right faith, right knowledge and right conduct, and all are connected.

Jains believe that every living being has a soul that passes through the cycles of life, death and rebirth. At the end of a lifetime the soul goes to a new body, depending on the life lived. Bad deeds drag the soul down to a lower form of life, while good deeds lift the soul up. The hope is that the perfected soul will break free of the painful cycle. Jains have no idea of a creator but, rather, understand the perfect soul as divine. The images in the temples, mostly of the *tirthankaras*, are not worshipped but venerated.

Some Jains live as monks and nuns, renouncing possessions, comfort and stability to become homeless wanderers who are reliant on alms. They may only travel on foot and some monks, of the Digambara Group, are completely naked. *Ahimsa* is the strict code of conduct of the monks and nuns so that, famously, as they walk they sweep the ground before them to make sure that they do not kill anything. They eat berries and fruits. Non-violence includes not only physical violence but also spoken and mental violence. *Ahimsa* includes positive acts of goodness to other living beings. *Ahimsa* is the first of the five vows taken by monks and nuns. The other vows are: speaking the truth, not taking anything, chastity, and non-attachment to people, places and things.

Secular Jains live in ordinary society and they also strive to live as non-violently as possible. They are strict vegans and many try to live as monks and nuns for a short period every day. They practise meditation. They work to develop tolerance of each other and of non-Jains. Listening to others is vitally important. They recognize that it is not always possible to do good and that there then may sometimes be a choice between a greater evil and a lesser evil. One of the festivals is Paryusana when all Jains ask forgiveness of anyone they may have injured in any way in the previous year. Jains fast in the days leading up to the festival. Fasting is frequently practised by Jains. They are very interested in ecological issues and environmental protection.

The Jain scriptures are many and varied. Some of the scriptures are the teachings of Mahavira and began orally. There are two traditions in Jainism, the Shvettambara and the Digambara traditions. The Digambara Jains believe that the early writings were lost, and their scriptures date from the second century CE while the Shvettambara Jains accept their scriptures from Mahavira's disciples. Ascetics have written texts over many centuries, and these are also accepted as part of the canon of scripture.

Above all, Jains strive to live disciplined lives. The lay members take vows of non-violence, non-stealing, chastity and non-acquisitiveness. They also practise mutual accountability.

Islam

There are approximately 1,118,243,000 Muslims in the world. Islam is a missionary religion and has spread from its original homeland in the Middle East to the Indian sub-continent, Africa, Malaysia, Indonesia, the Philippines and Europe.

In the UK today there are more than 1,500,000 Muslims. They began to arrive in the nineteenth century. Second and third groups arrived after World Wars One and Two. A fourth group arrived in the 1970s from Uganda and Kenya. The major centres of community are in most large towns, including Bradford, Birmingham, Preston and London. There are more than 600 mosques throughout the UK.

The Muslim religion developed in the seventh century CE following the birth of the prophet Mohammed in 570 CE. He was employed by Khadija to take her trading caravans to Syria and he later married her. During his long journeys he would have met Jews and Christians in the region. He received his first revelation in 610 CE. After that he began to preach the existence of the one God. He knew that the revelations were not his own but from God.

Gradually people heard his message and then a small community developed in Medina, from where the religion of Islam took shape. Mecca was captured and the Ka'aba, a cube built to house a meteorite, was cleansed.

Mohammed died in 632 CE and was succeeded by the four caliphs, who established Islam in most of the Middle East. Islam spread quickly and a hundred years after the death of Mohammed it had crossed North Africa as far as the Atlantic Ocean and into Spain. The Muslims occupied Persia and Afghanistan and crossed the River Indus.

The first four caliphs finalized the canon of the *Qu'ran*. They also began the collection of the *Hadith*, the history and stories of Mohammed. The strength of the Muslim community, begun during the time of Mohammed, was reinforced, and the *shahada* or witness of Islam, 'There is no God but Allah and Mohammed is his messenger', was established.

The *shahada* was the first of the 'Five Pillars of Islam', which give Muslims a structure for living and working. The other four pillars are: five daily hours for prayer; the payment of alms or *zakat* by all adult Muslims; the fast during the month of Ramadan, the month during which the first revelation of the Qu'ran was received; and the pilgrimage, the Haj, to Mecca and Medina, which Muslims in good health and with money for the journey have to undertake once in a lifetime.

Muslims accept the Qu'ran as the word of God, co-existent with him and preserved from eternity. The Qu'ran was revealed to Mohammed, first spoken and then written down in Arabic. Some Muslims believe that it should never be translated. It may be divided into two parts. The first part is of the early revelations from the early period in Mecca and is about God and his messenger. The second part includes the longer revelations from the time in Medina and includes reactions to some events, details of revelations and codes of practice. The Qur'an is wide ranging and does not recognize a separation between the sacred and the secular. Muslims read it as a spiritual exercise and treat it with great reverence. The question of contradictions is dealt with in the Qur'an itself, in surah 2.106, where it is explained that later verses may override earlier verses where they are contradictory. The earlier verse was not wrong, but was specific to a time or special context.

The 'sharia', Islamic law, was developed from the Qur'an, the Hadith and from consensus, *ijma*. There are differences in interpretation of the sharia between the four main legal schools.

The Sunni Muslims form approximately 90 per cent of the world's population of Muslims. Their name derives from the *sunnah*, the custom or the way in which the Prophet and his community lived and behaved. They accepted the four caliphs, chosen by the community from amongst Mohammed's tribe, as administrative leaders and guardians of Islam after Mohammed's death. They also accepted the subsequent dynasties of caliphs, who guarded the sharia. The last was the Sultan of the Ottoman Empire and the caliphate was abolished in 1924. The national governments of Muslim states were then expected to observe and guard the sharia. There are differences in devotional practice between different groups of Sunni Muslims. For example, the Deobandis, originating in India, place great emphasis on the Qur'an, the Hadith and the Hanafi legal traditions. The Barelwis, also from India, have a different focus and place great importance on devotion to Mohammed.

The Shi'a Muslims form 10 per cent of the Muslim population of the world. They believe that the leadership of the Islamic community should be hereditary. They believe that after the death of Ali, cousin of Mohammed, his two sons, Hassan and Husayn, began a line of imams which was chosen by Allah and which continues. They see the role and nature of the imam as very important spiritually, unlike the Sunni, who see the imam simply as a leader of prayers. Many of the Shi'a imams are charismatic. They also have authority to interepret the Qur'an and the law. The Shi'a are divided into different communities, depending upon how many and which imams are accepted as members of the original line, related, through Ali, to Mohammed.

The two main Shi'a groups are the Twelvers, who recognize twelve imams, and the Ismailis, who recognize seven imams. Since the sixteenth century the Twelver Shi'a have been the majority in Iran and their faith is the official religion. They are also the largest religious group in Iraq, where some of their most important shrines are situated. There are also communities in the subcontinent and in the Lebanon. Eleven of the twelve imams died violently, while the twelfth disappeared in 873 CE and the community waits for him to reappear. The Ismailis share with the Twelvers the acceptance of the first six imams descending from Ali, but disagree about the succession between two of the sons of the sixth imam. The Ismailis have been influenced by Greek philosophy and by an interpretation of history based on the number seven. They understand the Qur'an as having an outer and an inner interpretation. There are two major Ismaili groups, perhaps the best-known being the Nizaris whose spiritual leader is the Aga Khan. The Musta'lis believe in a hidden imam who is represented on Earth by their leader, the Da'i.

Sufism is Islamic mysticism. It is based on both the outer regulatory aspects of Islam and on inner spiritual elements. There are many Sunni and Shi'a Sufi orders whose members seek a path of devotion to God and purification. A famous Muslim who is still remembered and written about for her devotional insights is Rabi'a al-Adawiyya who lived in Baghdad in the eighth century CE. She addressed God as her beloved, her hope, her rest and her delight. Sufis understand that individual effort is itself not enough in striving towards God and that God himself gives the grace which makes the path towards intimacy with God possible. Sufis are ordinary Muslims and attend the mosque services. They have also developed other forms of worship including the reciting of the names of God and the singing of hymns. Some orders also use music and dance.

The Qur'an sees all people as worshippers and servants of God in every moment of their lives. Muslims understand body and spirit as inseparable during worship and they see the individual, as taught in the Qur'an, as part of the worshipping community. Prayer is the second pillar of Islam and there are five daily prayer times, each preceded by ritual washing. The prayers are communal on Fridays and would normally take place in the mosque, the place of prostration and of meeting. It is understood, however, that Muslims do not need a building in order to worship God. The worshippers face towards Mecca and pray, all over the world, as a single body.

Sikhism

There are 23,000,000 Sikhs worldwide today. The majority still live in the place of their origin, the Punjab. There are also Sikhs all over the world who remain linked to the Punjab, through their family ties, festivals and pilgrimages to special places. The central place of pilgrimage is the Golden Temple in Amritsar which is said to be like the lotus plant of devotion and good works growing from the clouded waters of life. It is memorably symbolic for the pilgrim, who is challenged to look beyond this world and towards God.

There are approximately 350,000 Sikhs in Britain, who form the largest Sikh community outside the Punjab. The main cultural and worship centre is Southall in west London and there are also strong Sikh communities in all the main cities, including Leeds, Bradford and Leicester.

The Sikh faith was founded by Guru Nanak, who was born in the Punjab in 1469 CE. He came to feel that his faith path was neither Hindu nor Muslim and went on to reject exclusivism in religion, including the caste system he was part of and also surrounded by. He taught that loving devotion and moral character were much more important than birth. He wrote his own beautiful hymns and stressed the need for each person to know God, who was everywhere, and to develop a good way of life. He offered a rich and life-affirming spirituality, including honest work, the giving of alms, cleanliness, devotion and service to God, the 'Formless', and to humanity. He taught that the aim of living was an inner transformation, leading to freedom from self and unity with the saints and with God.

The Sikh community grew in the area of the Punjab after Guru Nanak's death. Guru Nanak was followed by nine living successors, who were chosen for their spirituality. They taught in the vernacular and developed a strong religious community that faced many aggressors. Gradually Sikhs came to feel united in faith, in culture and as a people.

The last living guru was Guru Gobind Singh, who died in 1708 CE. He founded the order of the 'Khalsa' or community of the baptized following a long period of persecution under the Mughal Empire.

Vaisakhi is the festival that marks the formation of the Khalsa, the community of the initiated Sikhs that has developed around the five beloved ones who were prepared to die for the Guru. The Guru prepared *amrit*, a special drink for the five, who came originally from different castes, and who drank it from the same bowl. The men were given the name Singh and the women were given the name Kaur.

Guru Gobind Singh gave the distinctive external appearance to the Sikhs of the turban and the five sacred symbols – the uncut hair, the comb, the steel wristband, the shorts and the sword. He said that Sikhs should live according to a code of conduct, including the wearing of the five sacred symbols and, following baptism, abstinence from tobacco and alcohol. A male Sikh, whether baptized or not, is expected to wear the turban in public as a sign of his pride in his people and of his loyalty to them.

Guru Gobind Singh said that after his lifetime the Sikhs were to see their scriptures as their guide, so that the next and continuing guru was the book, the Guru Granth Sahib. The book is the collection of the words and hymns of Guru Nanak and of other gurus and holy men. Guru Gobind Singh added some of the words of his father, Guru Tegh Bahadur. The book was collected together by Guru Arjan, who is the largest single contributor, and in 1604 it was placed in the Golden Temple in Amritsar, which had been built by Guru Arjan. The Guru Granth Sahib is installed in every Sikh gurdwara around the world.

The Guru Granth Sahib has the central and honoured position in the gurdwara, normally being placed on a raised platform under a canopy, and it is cared for as a living guru. It is the only object for veneration within the gurdwara. Sikhs show devotion and offer respect on entry and again before worship begins. Any member of the congregation may read from the book during the worship and on special occasions it is read continuously from beginning to end. The poems and hymns will normally be sung by the people.

Every Sikh gurdwara has a kitchen and dining area and after worship the worshippers eat a communal meal. The gurdwara is thus a strong community and family centre. This tradition of the *langar* was introduced by the third guru, Amar Das. The *langar* is symbolic of the equality of all humanity. The meals are served freely to anyone who enters, an inspiring example of welcome, service and generosity.

The Baha'i faith

There are approximately six million Baha'is, in every country of the world except the Vatican, and with the largest number of people in India. Haifa in Israel is the home of the Baha'i world centre.

The British Baha'i community formed one of the first national spiritual assemblies in 1923. Today local communities are active all over the UK and there are more than 180 assemblies and approximately 6,000 Baha'is.

The Baha'i faith was founded by Bahau'llah, a Persian nobleman, in the 1860s CE in the midst of the Shi'a Islamic religion and culture. He had preached of religious reform and unity in Persia, taking the teachings of the Bab, a young Persian merchant who was martyred, as his inspiration. He called all people to turn to God and to live lives of piety and service. He spoke of the transcendent oneness of God and the essential oneness of the human race. He also spoke of the oneness that underlies all religion. He was arrested and spent time in a notorious dungeon. He and his family were then expelled from Persia in 1853, and so he travelled to Baghdad, Constantinople, Adrianople and Acre. He had announced his mission in 1863 and preached and wrote throughout his life. He died near Acre in 1892 when he was in his seventies.

After Bahau'llah's death the community was led by his eldest son, Abdu'l Baha, who shared his father's sufferings, including imprisonment in Turkey. On his release he travelled and preached. The Baha'i faith spread first in the East and then, towards the end of the nineteenth century, in the West, first in America and then in Europe. In 1911 and then in 1912–13 Abdu'l Baha visited the West, travelling to North America and then to Britain.

Abdu'l Baha died at Haifa in 1921 having chosen his grandson, Shogi Effendi, to guard the faith and interpret the scriptures. Shogi Effendi built up the administrative framework of the Baha'is. After he died in London in 1957 the Universal House of Justice was elected. This is an international body which is elected and which meets in the Baha'i world centre in Haifa.

The core of the Baha'i scriptures is the writings of Bahau'llah. The *Kitab-i-Aqdas* is 'the most holy book', and includes laws and social ordinances. The *Kitab-i-Iqan* is a book of theology. The 'Hidden Words' are spiritual and ethical teachings and the 'Seven Valleys' is a mystical work. Abdu'l Baha also wrote a lot, especially on the social teachings of the faith. His writings and the writings of the Bab are also included in the scriptures.

Baha'is believe that God is utterly transcendent and that there are individuals who reflect and manifest the attributes of God, who reveal the divine purpose for people on the Earth and who may make progress in religion. They recognize the main religious leaders of all the faiths but they have none of their own. They depend on the active involvement of their members. They meet in each other's homes to pray. There are also a few meeting houses.

The heart of the faith is the individual's relationship with God, the oneness of God, the oneness of religion and of all people, and the equality of men and women. Daily prayer and meditation are central and there is an annual 19-day fast. Baha'is also read from Bahau'llah's writings every morning and evening.

Baha'is work for universal education, including science, and the narrowing of the gap between the rich and the poor. They have initiated many development projects around the world, including health camps and tree-planting projects. Long-term projects include literacy work, farming and environmental projects. The Baha'i International Community is affiliated to the United Nations.

The houses of worship are beautifully designed and inspirational. They have been built on each continent. They are nine-sided and are the gift of the Baha'is to the world and its people, of all faiths and of none.

Appendix 1

Building good relations with people of different faiths and beliefs

As members of the human family we should show each other respect and courtesy. In our dealings with people of other faiths and beliefs this means exercising goodwill and:

- respecting other people's freedom within the law to express their beliefs and convictions;

- learning to understand what others actually believe and value, and letting them express this in their own terms;

- respecting the convictions of others about food, dress and social etiquette and not behaving in ways which cause needless offence;

- recognizing that all of us at times fall short of the ideals of our own traditions and never comparing our own *ideals* with other people's *practices*;

- working to prevent disagreement from leading to conflict;

- always seeking to avoid violence in our relationships.

When we talk about matters of faith with one another, we need to do so with sensitivity, honesty and straightforwardness. This means:

- recognizing that listening as well as speaking is necessary for a genuine conversation;

- being honest about our beliefs and religious allegiances;

- not misrepresenting or disparaging other people's beliefs and practices;

- correcting misunderstanding or misrepresentations not only of our own but also of other faiths whenever we come across them;

- being straightforward about our intentions;

- accepting that in formal interfaith meetings there is a particular responsibility to ensure that the religious commitment of all those who are present will be respected.

All of us want others to understand and respect our views. Some people will also want to persuade others to join their faith. In a multi-faith society where this is permitted, the attempt should always be characterized by self-restraint and a concern for the other's freedom and dignity. This means:

- respecting another person's expressed wish to be left alone;

- avoiding imposing ourselves and our views on individuals or communities who are in vulnerable situations in ways which exploit these;

- being sensitive and courteous;

- avoiding violent action or language, threats, manipulation, improper inducements or the misuse of any kind of power;

- respecting the right of others to disagree with us.

Living and working together is not always easy. Religion harnesses deep emotions which can sometimes take destructive forms. Where this happens, we must draw on our faith to bring about reconciliation and understanding. The truest fruits of religion are healing and positive. We have a great deal to learn from one another which can enrich us without undermining our own identities. Together, listening and responding with openness and respect, we can move forward to work in ways that acknowledge genuine differences but build on shared hopes and values.

This code was first published by the Inter Faith Network in 1993. © Inter Faith Network for the UK 1993, 2000.

Appendix 2

The 1993 declaration
'Towards a Global Ethic'

The world is in agony. The agony is so pervasive and urgent that we are compelled to name its manifestations so that the depth of this pain may be made clear.

Peace eludes us – the planet is being destroyed – neighbours live in fear – women and men are estranged from each other – children die!

This is abhorrent.

We condemn the abuses of Earth's ecosystems.

We condemn the poverty that stifles life's potential; the hunger that weakens the human body, the economic disparities that threaten so many families with ruin.

We condemn the social disarray of the nations; the disregard for justice which pushes citizens to the margin; the anarchy overtaking our communities; and the insane death of children from violence. In particular we condemn aggression and hatred in the name of religion.

But this agony need not be.

It need not be because the basis for an ethic already exists. This ethic offers the possibility of a better individual and global order, and leads individuals away from despair and societies away from chaos.

We are women and men who have embraced the precepts and practices of the world's religions:

- We affirm that a common set of core values is found in the teachings of the religions, and that these form the basis of a global ethic.

- We affirm that this truth is already known, but yet to be lived in heart and action.

- We affirm that there is an irrevocable, unconditional norm for all areas of life, for families and communities, for races, nations, and religions. There already exist ancient guidelines for human behaviour which are found in the teachings of the religions of the world and which are the condition for a sustainable world order.

We Declare:

We are interdependent. Each of us depends on the well-being of the whole, and so we have respect for the community of living beings, for people, animals, and plants, and for the preservation of Earth, the air, water and soil.

We take individual responsibility for all we do. All our decisions, actions, and failures to act have consequences.

We must treat others as we wish others to treat us. We make a commitment to respect life and dignity, individuality and diversity, so that every person is treated humanely, without exception. We must have patience and acceptance. We must be able to forgive, learning from the past but never allowing ourselves to be enslaved by memories of hate. Opening our hearts to one another, we must sink our narrow differences for the cause of the world community, practicing a culture of solidarity and relatedness.

We consider humankind our family. We must strive to be kind and generous. We must not live for ourselves alone, but should also serve others, never forgetting the children, the aged, the poor, the suffering, the disabled, the refugees, and the lonely. No person should ever be considered or treated as a second-class citizen, or be exploited in any way whatsoever. There should be equal partnership between men and women. We must not commit any kind of sexual immorality. We must put behind us all forms of domination or abuse.

We commit ourselves to a culture of non-violence, respect, justice, and peace. We shall not oppress, injure, torture, or kill other human beings, forsaking violence as a means of settling differences.

We must strive for a just social and economic order, in which everyone has an equal chance to reach full potential as a human being. We must speak and act truthfully and with compassion, dealing fairly with all, and avoiding prejudice and hatred. We must not steal. We must move beyond the dominance of greed for power, prestige, money, and consumption to make a just and peaceful world.

Earth cannot be changed for the better unless the consciousness of individuals is changed first. We pledge to increase our awareness by disciplining our minds, by meditation, by prayer, or by positive thinking. Without risk and a readiness to sacrifice there can be no fundamental change in our situation. Therefore we commit ourselves to this global ethic, to understanding one another, and to socially beneficial, peace-fostering, and nature-friendly ways of life.

We invite all people, whether religious or not, to do the same.

Notes

Inspire gratefully acknowledges the use of copyright items. Every effort has been made to trace copyright owners, but where we have been unsuccessful we would welcome information which would enable us to make appropriate acknowledgement in any reprint.

Introduction

1. Michael Ipgrave, ed., *The Road Ahead: A Christian–Muslim Dialogue*, London, Church House Publishing, 2002. Michael Ipgrave, ed., *Scriptures in Dialogue: Christians and Muslims Studying the Bible and the Qur'an Together*, London, Church House Publishing, 2004.

2. Kathryn Lum, 'Interreligious and Intercultural Dialogue in the Wake of 11 March: A portrait of the interfaith movement in Madrid', *Interreligious Insight*, Vol. 2, No. 3, July 2004, pp. 96-9.

Chapter 1

1. Marcus Braybrooke, *Pilgrimage of Hope: One Hundred Years of Global Interfaith Dialogue*, New York, Crossroad, and London, SCM, 1992.

2. Rabindranath Tagore, *Gitanjali*, London, Macmillan, 1913, p. 46.

3. *In Good Faith: The Four Principles of Interfaith Dialogue: A Brief Guide for the Churches*, Committee for Relations with People of Other Faiths, 1991. The booklet is available from Churches Together in Britain and Ireland, Third Floor, Bastille Court, 2 Paris Garden, London SE1 8ND.

4. The Faith Awareness Programme is the interfaith programme of Christians Aware.

5. *Religions in the UK: Directory 2002–3* is a guide to the faith communities, organizations and places of worship of the UK, published by the multi-faith centre at the University of Derby in association with the Inter Faith Network. The directory is regularly updated.

6. *Faith Offerings*, edited by Leicester Women for Inter Faith Understanding, Leicester, Christians Aware, 2005.

7. *Local Inter Faith Activity in the UK: A Survey*, Inter Faith Network, 2003.

8. *Inter Faith Cooperation, Local Government and the Regions: Councils of Faith as a Resource for the 21st Century*, Inter Faith Network, 2003.

9. A survey of local interfaith groups and councils is included in *Local Inter Faith Activity in the UK: A Survey*, Inter Faith Network, 2003.

10. The Inter Faith Network for the UK, 8A, Lower Grosvenor Place, London SW1W 0EN.

11. *Building Good Relations with People of Different World Faiths and Beliefs*, Inter Faith Network, 1993.

12. *Christians Aware* magazine, Summer 1998, p. 7.

13. Joy Barrow, ed., *Meeting Sikhs*, Leicester, Christians Aware, 1998, p. 114.

14. Barbara Butler and Jo White, *To Be a Pilgrim*, London, Kevin Mayhew, 2002, pp. 111–12.

15. Jonathan Sacks, 'The Jewish Community, Past, Present and Future', *Shap Journal*, 2001/2, p. 17.

16. Sacks, 'The Jewish Community', p. 19.

17. 'Nasreen', 'World Religions in Education', *Shap Journal*, 2001/2, p. 27.

18. Adi Granth 642.

19. Adi Granth 853.

20. *The Future of Multi-ethnic Britain*, Runnymede Trust Commission, London, Profile Books, 2000.

21. From a conference evaluation form, 1996.

22. Brahma Kumaris form an international spiritual university, led by women.

23. From a paper by Anne Wragg of the Concord Women's Friendship Group.

24. Tagore, *Gitanjali*, p. 42.

Chapter 2

1. Gwyneth Little, ed., *Meeting Hindus*, Leicester, Christians Aware, 2001, p. 69.

2. From *Connect: Different Faiths, Shared Values*, Inter Faith Network, 2004.

3. E. M. Forster, *The Hill of Devi*, Harmondsworth, Penguin, 1988.

4. Guru Granth Sahib, p. 679.

5. David Clark, 'A Pilgrimage to Sikh Holy Sites in the Punjab', *Christians Aware magazine*, Spring 2005, p. 34.

6. Little, *Meeting Hindus*, p. 62.

7. Little, *Meeting Hindus*, p. 64.

8. *The Gospel of the Lord Shri Krishna: The Bhagavad Gita*, trans. Shri Purohit Swami, London, Faber and Faber, 1978, p. 21.

9. Elizabeth J. Harris and Ramona Kauth, eds, *Meeting Buddhists*, Leicester, Christians Aware, 2004, p. 261.

10. Harris and Kauth, *Meeting Buddhists*, p. 262.

11. *Connect: Different Faiths, Shared Values*.

12. Aubrey Newman and Barbara Butler, eds, *A Sacred Memory: Lectures in Honour of Elchanan and Miriam Elkes*, School of Historical Studies, University of Leicester and Christians Aware, 2003, p. 28.

13. Newman and Butler, *A Sacred Memory*, p. 28.

Chapter 3

1. Paul Knitter, *No Other Name*, London, SCM, 1985. This book covers the views in detail. Alan Race, *Christians and Religious Pluralism: Patterns in the Christian Theology of Religions*, London, SCM, 1983.

2. Harris and Kauth, *Meeting Buddhists*, p. 252.

3. Graham Kings, *Christianity Connected*, Zoetermeer, Boeckencentrum, 2002, traces the development of Max Warren's theology of religions.

4. Kenneth Cragg, *Sandals at the Mosque: Christian Presence amid Islam*, London, SCM, 1959. General introduction to the Christian Presence Series.

5. A traditional Maasai prayer, given to the author by a Maasai friend.

6. Taken from *Nostra Aetate, the Declaration on the Relation of the Church to Non-Christian Religions.* Second Vatican Council, 1965.

7. Wesley Ariarajah, *Not without My Neighbour: Issues in Interfaith Relations*, Risk book series, WCC Publications 1999, gives details of the World Council of Churches' work with people of other faiths and of the Baar Declaration.

8. Abhishiktananda, *Hindu–Christian Meeting Point*, Delhi, ISPCK, 1969.

9. See Appendix 1.

10. Nadir Dinshaw, 'A Spiritual Journey', in *Sharing Ways and Wisdoms*, ed. Barbara Butler, London, Kevin Mayhew, 2001, p. 167.

11. Andrew Deuchar, ed., *A Last Embrace*, Harlech, Cairns Publications, 2003, p. 6.

12. Butler, *Sharing Ways and Wisdoms*, p. 179.

13. Marcus Braybrooke and Tony Bayfield, *Dialogue with a Difference: The Manor House Experience*, London, SCM, 1992.

14. Zadie Smith, *White Teeth*, Harmondsworth, Penguin, 2001.

15. R. S. Sugitharajah and Cecil Hargreaves, *Readings in Indian Christian Theology*, London, SPCK, 1993.

16. Vincent J. Donovan, *Christianity Rediscovered: An Epistle from the Maasai*, London, SCM, 1978.

17. *Din-Sevak: Verrier Elwin's Life of Service in Tribal India*, introduced by Dan O'Connor, published for the Christian Institute for the Study of Religion and Society, Bangalore, by ISPCK, Delhi, 1993.

Chapter 4

1. Oliver McTernan, *Violence in God's Name*, London, Darton, Longman & Todd, 2003, p. xiii.

2. Kristen Ashburn, interview, *The Telegraph* magazine, 15 November 2003.

3. Hala Jaber, 'The Avengers', news review, *The Sunday Times*, 7 December 2003.

4. Karen Armstrong, *The Battle for God: Fundamentalism in Judaism, Christianity and Islam*, London, HarperCollins, 2000.

5. *The Guardian*, 25 November 2003.

6. G. Vermes, *Jesus the Jew*, London, SCM, 1983. Braybrooke and Bayfield, *Dialogue with a Difference*.

7. Rosemary Radford Ruether, *Faith and Fratricide: The Theological Roots of Anti-Semitism*, New York, Seabury, 1974.

8. Aubrey Newman, *The Holocaust: We Must Never Forget, Nor Allow it to Happen Again*, London, Caxton Editions, 2002, is an excellent overview.

9. Martin Gilbert, *The Day the War Ended*, London, HarperCollins, 1995.

10. Najwa Farah, *A Continent Called Palestine*, London, SPCK, 1996.

11. Elias Chacour, *Blood Brothers*, Grand Rapids, Chosen Books, 1987.

12. Christian Aid Report, 'Losing Ground: Israel, Poverty and the Palestinians', 2003.

13. *The Guardian*, 15 September 2003.

14. *Islamophobia, a Challenge for Us All*, Runnymede Trust, 1997, available from 133 Aldersgate, London EC1A 4JA.

15. *Islamophobia: Issues, Challenges and Action*, a report by the Commission on British Muslims and Islamophobia, ed. Robin Richardson, Stoke on Trent, Trentham Books, 2004.

16. *The Guardian*, 11 August 2004.

17. *The Guardian*, 18 August 2004.

18. Monica Ali, *Brick Lane*, New York, Doubleday, 2003.

19. United Nations Population Division, *Faith Under Fire: A Report of the Second Class Citizenship and Intimidation of Christians in Pakistan*, 2002.

20. Akbar S. Ahmed, *Islam Today: A Short Introduction to the Muslim World*, London and New York, I. B. Taurus, 2001, p. 127.

21. *Faith Under Fire.*

22. Sanjay Trehan, 'I renounce religion', *Hindustan Times*, 5 March 2002.

23. *Christians Aware* magazine, Summer 2004.

24. Jamila Gavin, 'The story of Shiva', in Little, *Meeting Hindus*.

Chapter 5

1. From Gandhi's Talisman, in Mahatma Gandhi, *Last Phase*, vol. 2, 1958, p. 65.

2. Hans Küng, *Global Responsibility*, New York, Continuum, and London, SCM, 1991, p. 138.

3. His Holiness the Dalai Lama, 'Nobel Prize acceptance speech', in *Ocean of Wisdom*, San Francisco, Harper & Row, 1990.

4. Hans Küng, *Tracing the Way*, New York, Continuum, 2001.

5. Richardson, *Islamophobia: Issues, Challenges and Action*, p. 39.

6. See *Our Ministry and Other Faiths*, The Hospital Chaplaincies Council, Fielden House, Little College Street, London SWIP 3SH. See also *Hospital Chaplaincy and Other Faiths*, leaflet by the Committee for Other Faiths of the Roman Catholic Bishops' Conference, Park House, 6a Cresswell Park, London SE3 9RD. There are 18 leaflets which introduce other faiths and associated issues.

7. The organizations helping asylum seekers of all faiths include the Refugee Arrivals Project, Faith Asylum Refuge and the British Refugee Council.

8. *Gifts of Service to the World*, Parliament of the World's Religions, Cape Town, December 1999.

9. Visit the 'Food for Life' website at < www.ffl.org/html >

10. Taken from an unpublished document and quoted in Marcus Braybrooke, *Faith and Interfaith in a Global Age*, Grand Rapids and Oxford, CoNexus Press and Braybrooke Press, 1998, p. 85.

11. World Conference on Religion and Peace, UK & Ireland, 37 Grange Road, Bushey, Hertfordshire, WD2 2LQ.

12. Paul Knitter, *One Earth, Many Religions*, Maryknoll, NY, Orbis Books, 1995, pp. 79–80.

13. Knitter, *One Earth, Many Religions*, p. 80.

14. Martin Gilbert, *The Righteous*, New York, Doubleday, 2002.

15. Council of Christians and Jews, Drayton House, 30 Gordon Street, London WC1H 0AN.

16. See Marc H. Ellis, *Out of the Ashes*, London, Pluto Press, 2002.

17. Jeff Halper, *Obstacles for Peace*, Israeli Committee Against House Demolitions, 2004.

18. Jeff Halper, 'Honor Rachel: End House Demolitions', *Christians Aware* magazine, Spring 2003, p. 8.

19. Elias Chacour, *Blood Brothers*, Grand Rapids, Chosen Books, 1987, reprinted 2003. *Blood Brothers* is available from the Elijah Trust, 90 Denmark Street, Bedford MK40 3TJ. See also Elias Chacour, *We Belong to the Land*, San Francisco, Harper & Row, 1991.

20. The First Alexandria Declaration of the Religious Leaders of the Holy Land, 21 January 2002.

21. The Qur'an, 16.90.

22. *The Quest for Sanity: Reflections on September 11th and the Aftermath.* Muslim Council of Great Britain, 2002, xiii–xiv.

23. Barbara Butler, ed., *Open Hands: Reconciliation, Justice and Peace Work around the World*, Kevin Mayhew, 1998, p. 207.

24. From a Nipponzan Myohoji leaflet.

25. *Ashes and Light*, Nipponzan Myohoji, 1996, p. i.

26. Aung San Suu Kyi, 'Heavenly Abodes and Human Development', CAFOD, 1997.

27. His Holiness the Dalai Lama, *The Good Heart*, New York, Rider, 1996, pp. 38–39.

28. Address by His Holiness the Dalai Lama on his acceptance of the Nobel Peace Prize, 10 December 1989, Oslo, Norway.

29. Adam Curle, 'Reconciliation: Problems and Alternatives', in Butler, *Open Hands*.

30. See Desmond Tutu, *No Future without Forgiveness*, New York, Rider, 1999.

Chapter 6

1. *The Guardian*, 14 February 2003.

2. Source of statistics for this chapter: *Religions in the UK: Directory, 2002–3*, Multi-Faith Centre, University of Derby with the Inter Faith Network. The statistics are approximate.

Some questions and resources

The resources may be used as tools both before and after meeting people of other faiths and for developing understanding, trust and shared work.

Some questions to ask and discuss when reading and meeting

How are you responding to the challenge to find out more about other faiths?

When you meet people of other faiths do you discover that you have anything in common with them?

Does anything irritate you or clash with your own faith and culture in the course of your encounters with those who are different?

Have you experienced hospitality in the home of friends of another faith? If your answer is yes, how has this changed you?

What do you find that there is in common between the approaches of people of faith to worship and service?

Some useful resources

Akbar S. Ahmed, *Islam Today: A Short Introduction to the Muslim World*, London, I. B. Taurus, 1999.

An interesting and very useful survey.

Wesley Ariarajah, *Not without My Neighbour: Issues in Interfaith Relations*, Risk book series, World Council of Churches, 1999.

Joy Barrow, ed., *Meeting Sikhs*, Leicester, Christians Aware, 1998.

This book informs Christians about the main aspects of the Sikh religion. There are chapters on every aspect of Sikh life and on Sikh–Christian dialogue.

Colin Chapman, *Whose Holy City?*, Oxford, Lion, 2004.

The author looks at the history of Jerusalem and at its importance for Christians, Muslims and Jews. He suggests that if the problems of Jerusalem could be solved this would be a major step towards solving the problems of the Middle East.

Elizabeth Harris, ed., *Paths of Faith*, Leicester, Christians Aware, 2002.

This book gives a short introduction to the world faiths. The contributors are either adherents of the religion about which they write or have a close personal contact with the believers.

Elizabeth Harris and Ramona Kauth, eds, *Meeting Buddhists*, Leicester, Christians Aware, 2004.

The editors are a Christian and a Buddhist whose shared work has produced a beautiful, full-colour and informative book.

Maureen Henderson, *Friends Along the Way*, London, Epworth Press, 1999.

In Good Faith: The Four Principles of Interfaith Dialogue: A Brief Guide for the Churches, Committee for Relations with People of Other Faiths, from Churches Together in Britain and Ireland, 1991.

This small booklet is a useful tool for those who, having met people of other faiths, wish to develop friendship and shared work. It will give a wide range of Christians confidence that interfaith encounter and work are an essential part of Christian life in today's multicultural Britain and world.

Paul Knitter, *No Other Name*, London, SCM, 1985.

This is an excellent and detailed examination of the wide range of Christian views of the other world faiths.

Paul Knitter, *One Earth, Many Religions*, Maryknoll, NY, Orbis Books, 1995.

The author challenges people of all the world faiths to work together to relieve the sufferings of the world and to put their faith differences in second place to this urgent work.

Gwyneth Little, ed., *Meeting Hindus*, Leicester, Christians Aware, 2001.

There are 33 contributors to this book which, in full colour, offers an insight into the religious life of the people in prayer, worship, home, family, pilgrimage and much more.

Eric Lott, *Religious Faith, Human Identity: Dangerous Dynamics in Global and Indian Life*, Asian Trading Corporation and United Theological College, Bangalore, 2005.

This book is the 2000 Teape Lectures. It offers a deep insight into the interaction of faith and identity in the world, and especially in India.

Oliver McTernan, *Violence in God's Name*, London, Darton, Longman & Todd, 2003.

This is an excellent examination of religion and violence.

Christopher Partridge, ed., *The World's Religions*, Oxford, Lion, 2005.

This is an easily accessible and beautiful book which offers introductions to the histories, beliefs and practices of the world faiths. It is ideal as a reference book for individuals, church groups and schools.

Alan Race, *Christians and Religious Pluralism: Patterns in the Christian Theology of Religions*, London, SCM, 1983.

This is an introduction to Christian approaches to the other faiths.

Religions in the UK: Directory 2002–3, University of Derby and the Inter Faith Network.

This is an essential handbook for identifying faith communities in every area of the UK. It is a useful resource for local churches and libraries and for every person who wishes to meet people of other faiths. It is available from the Inter Faith Network.

Jonathan Sacks, *To Heal a Fractured World*, New York, Continuum, 2005.

Human beings have freedom and the challenge of this book is that it should lead to responsibility for the world and for those who are different, not to individualism.

Rabindranath Tagore, *Gitanjali*, London, Macmillan, Macmillan Pocket Tagore edition 1974, reprinted 1992.

Song/prayer offerings from one of the most famous poets in the world in the early twentieth century. It aids prayer and gives inspiration.

Some useful organizations

The Baha'i Information Office
27 Rutland Gate
London SW7 1PD

The Buddhist Society
58 Eccleston Square
London SW1 V 1PH

Christians Aware
Faith Awareness Programme
2 Saxby Street
Leicester LE2 0ND

Council of Christians and Jews
5th Floor, Camelford House
89 Albert Embankment
London SE1 7TP

Institute for Jewish Policy Research
79 Wimpole Street
London W1G 9RY

Inter Faith Network for the UK
8A Lower Grosvenor Place
London SW1W 0EN

The Islamic Foundation
Ratby Lane
Markfield
Leicester LE67 9RN

The Jain Centre
32 Oxford Street
Leicester LE1 5XU

The Muslim College
20–22 Creffield Road
London W5 3RP

National Council of Hindu Temples
c/o Shree Sanatan Mandir
Weymouth Street
Off Catherine Street
Leicester LE4 6FP

The Sikh Missionary Society
10 Featherstone Road
Southall
Middlesex UB2 5AA

World Congress of Faiths
London Inter Faith Centre
125 Salisbury Road
London NW6 6RG

World Zoroastrian Organisation
135 Tennison Road
South Norwood
London SE25 5NF